PREPARING SCH SCHOOL SYSTEMS FOR THE 21ST CENTURY

Council of 21
John Glenn, Honorary Chair
Report on the Mount Vernon Conference

Frank Withrow
with Harvey Long and Gary Marx

This millennial project was made possible through support from AMP Incorporated and the Electric Power Research Institute. A distinguished Council of 21, a Council of Advisers, and representatives of gravity-breaking school systems generously contributed their thoughts and ideas, which form the basis for this study. Senator John Glenn served as Honorary Chair.

AMERICAN ASSOCIATION OF SCHOOL ADMINISTRATORS

American Association of School Administrators
1801 N. Moore Street
Arlington, VA 22209
(703) 875-0748
http://www.aasa.org

Copyright ©1999, American Association of School Administrators
ISBN: 0-87652-235-5
Library of Congress Catalog Card No.: 98-74779
AASA Stock No.: 234-002

Printed in the United States of America.

To order additional copies, call AASA's Order Fulfillment Department at 1-888-782-2272 (PUB-AASA) or, in Maryland, call 1-301-617-7802.

Note: The views expressed in *Preparing Schools and School Systems for the 21st Century* do not necessarily reflect the official positions of the American Association of School Administrators or its members; AMP Incorporated and the Electric Power Research Institute; the individual views of members of the Council of 21, Council of Advisers, and gravity-breaking school systems; nor the Honorary Chair. Most attributions are based on comments made during the Mount Vernon Conference or in response to the two-round survey conducted as a part of this study. Some other attributions, noted as such, are the views expressed by various experts in print or interviews.

Preparing Schools and School Systems for the 21st Century

Preface

New centuries and new millennia are times for taking stock and for looking ahead. As we enter the 21st century and the third millennium, we are encountering some of the most profound and rapid changes the world has ever seen. Many of these changes are driven by technology, others by our personal and shared values.

Educators face a daunting challenge. That is why the central focus of *Preparing Schools and School Systems for the 21st Century* has been the identification of *characteristics of schools and school systems capable of preparing students for a global knowledge/ information age.*

While schools have done a masterful job of preparing students for the industrial age, we are moving at warp speed into a whole new era. The future of our nation and of the world depends on our ability to lead and to adapt as we prepare students to turn the infinite information available to them into knowledge, and eventually into wisdom.

At AASA, we do not see this study and its conclusions as the last word. Instead, we believe this study suggests a bridge from what our schools and school systems are to what they need to become. We urge school leaders and the communities they serve, across the United States and in other countries, to review this powerful publication, and to use it to make positive and profound changes that will help us better prepare our children for the future.

Paul D. Houston
Executive Director
American Association of School Administrators

JOHN GLENN
OHIO

COMMITTEES:
• GOVERNMENTAL AFFAIRS
• ARMED SERVICES
• SELECT COMMITTEE ON INTELLIGENCE
• SPECIAL COMMITTEE ON AGING

United States Senate

WASHINGTON, DC 20510–3501

February 17, 1998

American Association of School Administrators
1801 North Moore Street
Arlington, VA 22209

Dear Friends:

It is my privilege to serve as Honorary Chair of the Council of 21 for the American Association of School Administrators. While I regret that I am unable to join you today, I want to take this opportunity to emphasize the value of conferences such as these to the youth of our nation.

The young people of today are doubly challenged to reach out - not just beyond the physical confines of the planet and the limits of present knowledge, but also beyond the confining prejudices of the past. To meet these demands, young people must be prepared with excellent educations and advanced skills. Your proactive efforts to prepare our young people for the global information age will ensure America's competitiveness in the 21st Century. I am hopeful for the future of our nation because of people like you – who are committed to helping prepare today's youth for tomorrow's challenges.

Please accept my sincere thanks for everyone's participation at this conference, and my best wishes for a productive and rewarding future.

Best regards.

Sincerely,

John Glenn
United States Senator

JG/cb

PREPARING SCHOOLS AND SCHOOL SYSTEMS FOR THE 21ST CENTURY

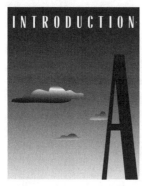

Dynamic Process for Creating a New Education System

Preparing Schools and School Systems for the 21st Century is not an attempt to dictate the shape of our education system. Instead, it is designed to stimulate discussion and debate in communities across the nation and in other parts of the world about the characteristics of schools and school systems capable of preparing students for a global knowledge/information age.

In 1996, the American Association of School Administrators, working with a distinguished Council of 55, identified the academic knowledge, skills, and behaviors students would need to be ready for the future. That study, *Preparing Students for the 21st Century,* continues to draw worldwide attention. However, concern is growing that our education system, which has done a remarkable job of preparing students for an industrial age, now must itself be reshaped as we move into an entirely new era.

This study, which took place during 1998, the 15th anniversary year of "A Nation at Risk," is the result of a process perhaps more rigorous than many previous historic studies.

Most studies and their subsequent reports either tell us what is wrong with the present system of education or prescribe a few fixes. In our view, the time has come to put discussions of fixing the system to rest and to take a look at the kind of system we need to take us into the future. Indeed, that is the philosophy that has driven this year-long project.

Preparing Schools and School Systems for the 21st Century was made possible by the contributions of AMP Incorporated and the Electric Power Research Institute. These organizations have not only demonstrated their social responsibility and their commitment to improving the lives of children and the quality of education, but they have also made available their substantial intellectual and material resources to aid us. They have become true partners, and yet, from the beginning, they have relinquished any editorial control, insisting instead that this study reflect the outcome of this millennial effort.

The Process

The process that has culminated in this publication began with the appointment of a prestigious Council of 21 (see page 100), composed of leaders in business, government, education, and other walks of life. Senator John Glenn agreed to serve as Honorary Chair. The Council met in an all-day technologically sophisticated and highly motivated session on February 17, 1998, at historic Mount Vernon, home our first U.S. President. At that meeting, the Council of 21 identified more than 200 "characteristics of schools and school systems capable of preparing students for a global knowledge/ information age." The Council's work was limited only by requirements calling for equal opportunity and the need to prepare students for life in a democratic society.

Following the Mount Vernon Conference, the characteristics were vetted through a two-round quasi-Delphi process. The Council of 21 was augmented by a similar group, known as the Council of Advisers (see page 102), and representatives of more than 20 "Gravity-Breaking" schools and school systems (see page 104) who helped us place the characteristics in priority, determine their possible impact, suggest when if ever they would become commonplace, and point out items that may have been overlooked at the Mount Vernon meeting.

Survey results were tabulated using a weighted formula that considered not only the suggested priority, but also the potential impact of each characteristic.

Perspective

To place this study in perspective, we want to be clear that it is what it is, the collected thinking of an outstanding group of Americans willing to express their views about the future of education. They represent many parts of our nation, many professions, and many walks of life.

As you review this report of the Council of 21, you'll find that *Chapter 1* presents 16 major characteristics developed after a thorough review of the entire study. *Chapters 2 through 11* review specific characteristics identified in each of 12 categories. These chapters present explanations of 8 or more characteristics rated highest in our survey. *Chapter 12* offers suggestions about how school leaders might put this dynamic study to work in their communities. *Additional information* in this publication includes a section devoted to special challenges, a historic perspective, and lists of those who participated in this effort.

Throughout, you'll find comments from members of the Council of 21, Council of Advisers, and representatives of gravity-breaking schools and school systems as well as others. The conclusion of most chapters or sections includes a listing of additional characteristics identified by the Council of 21

2

that ranked lower in our study than those discussed in detail. Time and space limitations kept us from discussing these characteristics, but they too are important and, in many cases, are similar to those discussed.

Presenting a Beginning

The publication of *Preparing Schools and School Systems for the 21st Century* is not the end of this project. In fact, it is the beginning, as education systems across the nation and in other parts of the world jump the curve, break out of the box, and put their creative genius to work in deciding, one community at a time, how we can effectively prepare our students for life in a global knowledge/information age.

16 CHARACTERISTICS OF SCHOOLS AND SCHOOL SYSTEMS FOR THE 21ST CENTURY

The following are characteristics of schools and school systems capable of preparing students for a global knowledge/information age. They are not in order of priority. All are important.

- The definitions of "school," "teacher," and "learner" are reshaped by the digital world.

- All students have equal opportunity for an outstanding education, with adequate funding, no matter where they live.

- Educators are driven by high expectations and clear, challenging standards that are widely understood by students, families, and communities.

- A project-based "curriculum for life" engages students in addressing real-world problems, issues important to humanity, and questions that matter.

- Teachers and administrators are effectively prepared for the global knowledge/information age.

- Students, schools, school systems, and communities are connected around-the-clock with each other and with the world through information-rich, interactive technology.

- School systems conduct, consider, and apply significant research in designing programs that lead to constantly improving student achievement.

- Students learn to think, reason, and make sound decisions and demonstrate values inherent in a democracy.

4

- School facilities provide a safe, secure, stimulating, joyous learning environment that contributes to a lifelong passion for learning and high student achievement.

- Leadership is collaborative, and governance is focused on broad issues that affect student learning.

- Students learn about other cultures, respect and honor diversity, and see the world as an extended neighborhood.

- Schools promote creativity and teamwork at all levels, and teachers help students turn information into knowledge and knowledge into wisdom.

- Assessment of student progress is more performance based, taking into account students' individual talents, abilities, and aspirations.

- A student-centered, collaboratively developed vision provides power and focus for education communitywide.

- Continuous improvement is a driving force in every school and school system.

- Schools are the crossroads and central convening points of the community.

Council of 21
American Association of
School Administrators

Characteristics of Schools and School Systems for the 21st Century

The only way to coast is downhill. This is especially true in education. We're expected to prepare our students for a world we may never see and about which we can only dream. That means we need to anticipate the future. Some say we need to stay ahead of the curve. Actually, we need to use our experience, our creativity, and the wisdom of the ages to think outside the box, to see things in a whole new light, and ultimately not just to stay ahead of the curve, but to jump it. We must use what we know not as a resting point but as a launching pad as we design schools capable of educating our students for a new century and a new millennium.

Schools and school systems in the United States have done a noteworthy job of preparing students for the industrial age; fewer have systematically decided how they will prepare students for the 21st century. Therefore, if we continue on our present path, we'll be preparing students for a world that will no longer exist.

Our central question in *Preparing Schools and School Systems for the 21st Century* has been:

What are the characteristics of schools and school systems capable of preparing students for a global knowledge/information age?

After scanning the results of the entire study, we have identified what we believe are some of the primary characteristics of schools and school systems capable of doing just that.

The 16 overriding characteristics or drivers identified by this study represent common themes, based on the work of our Council of 21, Council of Advisers, and representatives of gravity-breaking schools and school systems. Their purpose is not to paint a picture of the perfect school system for the 21st century. Instead, we hope these characteristics will help drive discussion and debate as communities reshape their schools and school systems to even better serve all students and prepare them for life in not only a new century, but a new millennium.

Common Themes: 16 Characteristics of Schools and School Systems Capable of Preparing Students for a Global Knowledge/Information Age

- **The definitions of "school," "teacher," and "learner" are reshaped by the digital world.**

In the past, when we've used the term "school" we have generally thought of a building. While buildings will continue to be very important, the term "school" must take on an expanded meaning far beyond the physical structure in the 21st century. "School" will become even more encompassing, embracing communities of knowledge and learning that are interest-wide, communitywide, and worldwide. While there may always be a school building, it must differ in design and purpose. A school will likely become more like a nerve center that connects teachers, students, and the community to the wealth of knowledge that exists in the world.

Consistent with the evolving design and purpose of schools, the term "teacher" must earn and take on a mantle of even greater professionalism. Teachers will become orchestrators of learning because students will have access to a world of information through the Internet and many other sources. Teachers will need to become facilitators and moderators as well as purveyors of vast amounts of knowledge and subject matter specialists. According to our Council of Advisers, "Teachers need to understand the subject they teach and be able to get it across to students." At the same time, they need to be able to put that information and knowledge into a broader context and nudge their students toward wisdom.

In too many cases, education has focused on the needs of adults in the system rather than on students. Out of both necessity and curiosity, lifelong learning must become a part of people's lives as we move into the 21st century. As we consider the term "learner," we need to think about preparing students for life in the real world. We need to be more flexible in how we teach because students have different interests and talents. If we don't help every student develop to his or her potential, we will pay the price of neglect. The simple fact is, we can't afford to lose a single child.

- **All students have equal opportunity for an outstanding education, with adequate funding, no matter where they live.**

The system of education in the United States is decentralized. The level of wealth varies from one community to the next. Therefore, as we approach the new millennium, the amount individual school districts spend per student might range from $2,000 to $20,000. While the Council of 21 made clear that equal funding is not necessarily tantamount to equal opportunity, its findings reflect the view that our country cannot afford to divide or sort students based on their parents' educational, social, or economic characteristics.

Equal opportunity must be a philosophy that drives everything from funding to the expectations we have for our students. As one member of the Council says, "Teachers should bring out the best in their students no matter what or how it is done. That also applies to individuals with disabilities, the disadvantaged, and the legions of children who may have just recently arrived from other countries."

- **Educators are driven by high expectations and clear, challenging standards that are widely understood by students, families, and communities.**

The standards and expectations we set must help prepare students for a global knowledge/information age. Standards often seem bureaucratic and are sometimes seen as an external force. On the other hand, expec-

tations seem closer to the student, more of an internal force. Schools and school systems will need to reflect a proper balance of both. And both need to be widely understood and enthusiastically developed and embraced by students, educators, families, business/government representatives, and communities. Schools simply can't do the job alone.

According to one member of the Council of 21, "Everyone, including the student, must expect the best." Another Council member adds, "Standards and expectations must be high but realistic, based on research and experience." And according to a teacher on the Council, "Schools, teachers, and students need to be part of the process of developing the standards and expectations. It should not be a top-down process." As a group, the Council of 21 makes clear that there should be no upper limits placed on learning and achievement.

- **A project-based "curriculum for life" engages students in addressing real-world problems, issues important to humanity, and questions that matter.**

The Council of 21 forcefully states that students must be able to connect what they are learning with what is happening or may happen in the real world. Teachers will be challenged to help students make that connection— to explain to students why what they're learning has value. One Council member offers, "Life is complicated today, and even our college graduates sometimes lack practical skills they need in everyday life."

The Council also reaffirms what our earlier study, *Preparing Students for the 21st Century,* pointed out—that students need to be prepared in liberal studies, including but not limited to math, science, literature, the arts, culture, history, civics, philosophy, and communications skills. Students will need to be prepared for responsible citizenship in a democracy. They must develop characteristics of goodness and learn to treat other people well. Participation in the arts should help students develop their creative talents, and our approach to education should encourage students to think "outside the box." Students should emerge from our schools with perseverance and curiosity as well as a grounding in an expanding list of "the basics." In short, education must be relevant to the needs of people who will live their lives in the new century.

- **Teachers and administrators are effectively prepared for the global knowledge/information age.**

It goes almost without saying that in the 21st century all teachers and administrators must be prepared to make the best possible use of technology, both for student learning and for school and school district efficiency.

Because of the Internet, many students in a class may have more information about some subjects than the teacher. That basic fact could have a profound effect on how we prepare our teachers. Tomorrow's teachers must become much more

In 1991, the U.S. Labor Department Secretary's Commission on Achieving Necessary Skills (SCANS) released a report on what students would need to know and be able to do in the future. Briefly, the report concluded that:

- All American high school students must develop a new set of competencies and foundation skills if they are to enjoy a productive, full, and satisfying life.

- The qualities of high performance that today characterize our most competitive companies must become the standard for the vast majority of our companies, large and small, local and global.

- The nation's schools must be transformed into high-performance organizations in their own right.

than dispensers of information. They must be able to guide students as they turn information into knowledge and then turn that knowledge into wisdom. The Council of 21 predicts that teachers will serve as facilitators, moderators, and role models, as well as purveyors of wisdom and subject matter specialists—a formidable challenge.

Ultimately, in the 21st century school system, teachers and administrators need to move beyond managing time and space to managing for results.

- **Students, schools, school systems, and communities are connected around-the-clock with each other and with the world through information-rich, interactive technology.**

The word "community" is taking on new meaning. Electronic networks are pulling all of us together. The late Marshall McLuhan, who coined the term "Global Village," said a community is a group of people who share common information, common feelings, and common goals. With new technologies, communities extend far beyond neighborhoods or school attendance areas to encompass anyone who is interested in a certain issue or topic. We are virtually connected to the world.

Schools and school systems, if they haven't already, must begin developing web pages and communicating with parents and the community via e-mail. Their sophistication in using these interactive vehicles will skyrocket. As we prepare schools and school systems for the 21st century, our Council of 21 calls for equal access to technology by students and teachers, both at home and at school. All schools should be connected to electronic networks, and teachers should learn how to use new technologies as learning tools.

Students will do more self-learning and know how to access certain information resources without the immediate help of teachers. Schools will use electronic networks to get parents and the community on the education team. The school system web site will carry everything from the daily lunch menu to tips on parenting and homework assignments.

Again, we need to be concerned about equal opportunity. We must avoid developing classes of people such as the technology-rich and the technology-poor. To deal with equity concerns, some schools are allowing students to check out computers or making them available at libraries and other sites in the community. Schools and school systems must develop even more inventive ways for addressing problems posed by the "digital divide."

- **School systems conduct, consider, and apply significant research in designing programs that lead to constantly improving student achievement.**

It's a fact that business and industry spend a great deal more on research and development than we do in education. And our critics tell us that much of the research conducted in education has little relationship to actually improving student learning.

The Council of 21 concludes that schools and school systems in the 21st century must do even more research focused on improving student achievement and must use that research as part of the decision-making process. The Council calls for even greater attention to the physiology of learning, including research into brain development. Council members want to see teachers taking a more active role in research, strengthened by training that will help them interpret and apply significant research in the classroom.

- **Students learn to think, reason, and make sound decisions and demonstrate values inherent in a democracy.**

In every part of this study, the Council tells us that critical thinking, higher-level thinking, and decision-making skills are basic to a sound education, and that those skills must penetrate every area of the curriculum.

As one member of the Council puts it, simply knowing how to think isn't enough. Students need to become resourceful and creative. They need to apply their thinking and reasoning skills in every subject, whether it is literature, the arts, culture, history, or math.

In our earlier study devoted to what students would need to know and be able to do to be prepared for the 21st century, one thing came through in virtually every area we examined. It was the need to help students become more civil, understand and become participants in a free and democratic society, understand the consequences of their own actions and how their actions affect others, understand the need for a code of ethics, and to be good people who are honest, respectful, trustworthy, and caring. Students need to understand rights, but they need also to understand and exercise responsibilities basic to maintaining those rights. It is up to school systems to help instill these attributes in them.

- **School facilities provide a safe, secure, stimulating, joyous learning environment that contributes to a lifelong passion for learning and high student achievement.**

AASA's Executive Director Paul Houston says students should be as excited about school the day they graduate as they were the day they entered kindergarten.

When discussing facilities, the Council of 21 addressed the learning environment, school climate, and the school building itself, what some call "the building envelope." Council members assert that the school's climate must reflect a joy and passion for learning, and students must feel safe and secure. Abraham Maslow and others have called attention to the need for safety and security, and effective schools research has confirmed the imperative of a safe and orderly environment in education.

The walls, floors, and ceilings of a school should not be barriers. Instead, they should hold wires and connections that put the school in touch with the community and the world. The buildings themselves should be up-to-date, clean, and appropriately lighted, with proper temperature and air quality control. They should be places where students want to be.

As a test, educators should sit down in the outer office of their schools and ask if it is the type of place they would like to bring their child to be educated. Is there a sense of warmth? Do people treat each other well? Is there a feeling of excitement? Do people respect each other? Those are the same things parents and others in the community observe when they come into a school.

- **Leadership is collaborative, and governance is focused on broad issues that affect student learning.**

Rather than making major decisions in isolation, administrators must ask the opinions of teachers, parents, and others on the staff and in the community. The Council of 21 also reminds us that part of the challenge administrators will face is the management of expectations. What can people logically expect of their schools? What shouldn't they expect? Working with students, staff, parents, and the community, administrators need to clarify expectations and make sure those expectations are broadly understood.

Also, teachers and principals must have enough flexibility and control to effectively run their own schools and classrooms. School district administration will likely move even further in the direction of facilitation and capacity building and away from command and control. District-level administrators will work toward making the school system the crossroads of the community, and they, themselves, will become primary conveners of the community, connecting people and resources to get the job done. Collaboration will be central to truly effective management of schools and school systems.

In the United States, school boards are generally elected by the people. The Council urges those boards to focus on the common goal of providing a good education for all students, and not on individual special interests such as firing a teacher or censoring books. While the line between policy and administration will always be gray, the general direction in the new century should be toward school boards playing a progressive policy role as members of the community's education leadership team.

What we need, according to our Council, are school systems and communities where people are willing and able to say, "We're all in this together."

- **Students learn about other cultures, respect and honor diversity, and see the world as an extended neighborhood.**

The United States is a microcosm of the world. It's not uncommon to find school systems whose students speak 40 or 50 languages, reflect dozens of cultures, and come from many parts of the world. The Council of 21 asserts that educators and communities must help each student understand and appreciate the beauty of other cultures and to respect all people. Students must have a solid grounding in the principles of human rights. They must understand people who hold different values and learn to accept dissent and individual differences. It is possible, even given our heterogeneity, to reach mutual understanding.

Our motto in the United States is E Pluribus Unum, "Of the many...One!" We need to reflect that in what we teach and how we teach it. A school is the place where all students come together for a common experience. It is at school that students can learn other languages and experience the strength of diversity.

According to our Council, our schools need to embody the principles of a democratic society for all students and adults. Therefore, we must model democratic principles and respect for diversity in the way we run our schools and school systems.

- **Schools promote creativity and teamwork at all levels, and teachers help student turn information into knowledge and knowledge into wisdom.**

Preparing Students for the 21st Century states that students must be able to work with others as we move into the new century. While we need people who will take individual initiative, we also need the synergy and collective thinking that comes from collaboration. Most business and professional people have already declared teamwork and creativity survival skills. In the 21st century, teamwork involving students, staff, and community must become commonplace. These teams will work together face-to-face as well as electronically.

There are cautions here. The same computers that can unite us in a community of interest can also isolate us if we look only at a computer screen and seldom interact face-to-face with people.

As we've mentioned, students now have access to information from all over the world. The Council of 21 notes that the teacher's role will change dramatically from dispensing information to working alongside students helping them apply that information as knowledge and eventually turn it into wisdom. Truly outstanding teachers have always taken this approach.

- **Assessment of student progress is more performance based, taking into account students' individual talents, abilities, and aspirations.**

As states have assumed an increased role in funding education, most state legislatures have called for more tests to determine whether the investment of state tax dollars in education is paying off. With growing international competition, we are also seeing an increasing demand for more national testing. All of these tests are in addition to the local tests schools administer on a day-to-day basis.

As we move toward a new century, concern is growing about whether schools are required to spend too much time testing. As some people have pointed out, you can't fatten a calf simply by weighing it all the time. You need some time to actually feed it.

The Council of 21 cautions that as we set standards and develop assessments we not freeze the education system while the world is changing so quickly around it. Flexibility is needed. Some students, for example, may be able to achieve in areas that go far beyond the formal, taught curriculum. It may be those students who light our way into the future. Schools, therefore, must be cautious not to trim students down to size and assume that one size fits all.

- **A student-centered, collaboratively developed vision provides power and focus for education communitywide.**

The Council of 21 emphasizes that truly enlightened leaders in education must develop a vision for education in their communities, and must bring educators, parents, and others together to help them do it. Administrators must be open to what staff and community can teach them and must become masters of collaboration, while ensuring the intellectual and moral integrity of the school and school system. On top of that, school systems and their leaders need to know, through surveys, advisory groups, and just plain listening, what constituents know, what they don't know, and what they need to know to give schools their support.

A major concern is keeping the focus of the community on issues that make a difference in student learning rather than falling victim to the distractions. Robert Spillane, a former AASA National Superintendent of the Year, is known for saying that for him, as a school leader, "The main thing is to keep the main thing the main thing."

- **Continuous improvement is a driving force in every school and school system.**

Our Council of 21 unequivocally states that educators cannot let the system stiffen or become atrophied in our fast-changing world. Evaluations every 3 to 5 years may not be good enough. Planning must be a continuous process. Educators must monitor programs every day and make improvements on a day-to-day, even minute-by-minute, basis. Schools and school systems must also monitor how students, their parents, and the community feel about the school. The principles of quality management clearly apply here.

- **Schools are the crossroads and central convening point of the community.**

Everything that happens in a school affects the community, and everything that happens in the community has implications for the schools. The Council of 21 describes schools as around-the-clock hubs for lifelong learn-

14

ing. Schools will be the connecting point for education and achievement for all who live and work in the community in the next century. They will likely become centers for other services, such as healthcare, housing, social, and other community services and agencies. Some already are. A few school systems have set up classrooms and even whole public schools in office buildings. Schools are also allowing business and community organizations to use facilities for ongoing employee training. While growing numbers of schools provide services for older citizens, some are predicting that schools will eventually provide a site for geriatric care, along with child care, as the baby boom generation moves into retirement.

Because many communities have homes in which both parents are working, and because many have an increasing number of "empty nesters," school systems must become even more creative at getting people involved. The Council of 21 contends that everyone in the community should be on the education team. Schools simply can't do it alone — in any century.

CHAPTER 2

Contemporary Technology

CHARACTERISTICS

- Technology is used as an integral learning tool.
- All schools and classrooms are fully connected to electronic networks of information.
- All teachers and students have equal access to technology at home and school, with adequate support.
- Technology is used to create greater efficiency and effectiveness in learning.
- School systems use technology to enhance planning and other functions.
- Technology is used in schools to expand the nature and boundaries of knowledge.
- All children are engaged in continuous self-learning and know how to access information sources without the immediate help of teachers.
- Teachers have minimum competency requirements in technology for recertification and must give evidence of its integrated use in classrooms.
- Technology opens the door to self-directed learning.
- Distance learning is extensively used to deliver inservice staff development.

Educators ... are discovering that this unique technology has the potential to teach as well as thrill.

David Field, *Teacher Magazine*, May/June 1998

The military and NASA have been leaders in using technology for training. For example, virtual reality is used in the training of military and commercial pilots. At the United Airlines training facilities in Denver, pilots engage in simulated landings and take-offs using different aircraft and a wide range of weather conditions at most of the world's airports.

As we move out of the 20th century, technology has become a magnet for legions of young people. They are fascinated by its potential, whether surfing the web, chatting with a newfound friend half a world away, playing a video game, or doing schoolwork. In the 21st century, we can expect simulations and other technologically driven learning tools to find a home in our nation's classrooms.

K–12 educators will be challenged to take advantage of contemporary technologies to enhance and expand the learning of all children. Nancy Stover, president of Your Choice TV, says, "It is inevitable that technology will provide students with a rich, multicultural learning experience."

There are several essential aspects of technology that educators should consider incorporating in schools, among them: up-to-date technology to build management systems that can track individual student progress, intelligently developed software to provide students with real-world experiences not possible in the traditional school, 21st century technology-based assessment tools, and telecommunications technology that provides access to multiple-tiered digital libraries.

Just as paper and pencils replaced slate boards in schools, contemporary information and communications technologies are either replacing or enhancing a number of traditional resources.

> *"The change from atoms to bits is irrevocable and unstoppable."*
>
> Nicholas Negroponte in *Being Digital*

As we move into a new era, our economic opportunities and perhaps our survival as a nation will depend on our ability to take a lead in the development and effective use of technology. Schools must play a central role in meeting this challenge.

The following are among the characteristics of schools and school systems capable of preparing students for the 21st century in the area of technology, as identified by the Council of 21:

- **Technology is used as an integral learning tool.**

Some educators have referred to computers and other contemporary technologies as imagination machines. They are the magic carpets that allow students to explore the world in virtual reality. Learners can experience sights, sounds, and text. They can manipulate things in both macro and micro permutations. It is mind-boggling to think about what it means that elementary students can now graph complex equations and observe graphically the interrelationships of variables in the equation. The University of Wisconsin has demonstrated that very young students with these tools can perform at high school and even college levels.

"I have seen the power of these new technologies at work, and we need to blend them with our other learning tools," says Grace Williams, a teacher at Carter G. Woodson Elementary School in Jacksonville, Fla., and a Florida Teacher of the Year. Monica Bradsher of MPB Associates in Alexandria, Va., suggests that these technologies should "not only be an integral learning tool, but also integrated into the curriculum."

As we move into the 21st century, all schools must have just-in-time desktop printing facilities that enable them to provide individualized books for students. Just-in-time additions to individual books can be provided as the student meets his or her performance objectives. Also, all students must have access to digital resources in their classrooms, homes, and libraries.

- **All schools and classrooms are fully connected to electronic networks of information sources.**

As new information resources become ubiquitous in society, they must also find their way into schools and classrooms. In the 21st century, schools will be in a race to simply keep up with technologies that are quickly becoming commonplace in many students' homes. Schools will constantly be challenged to plan for long-term acquisition, installation, operation, maintenance, and replacement or upgrading of these systems, which create virtual windows to the world.

"A major question school systems will face will relate to how they access information," Bradsher remarks. "Will it mean the installation of fiber-optic cables? Will every desk have Internet accessibility? Will schools use broadband?"

As schools head into the new millennium, they will also be confronted with an unresolved argument about online safety, balancing the fact that some web sites may offer certain things they don't particularly want students to see against First Amendment concerns. A further concern is the need for funding and other support to get all schools connected and to provide the software and training teachers need to make the most of these new and exciting learning resources.

- **All teachers and students have equal access to technology at home and school, with adequate support.**

As one step in introducing new technologies, some schools have given it first to the teachers, enabling them to get comfortable with it. Schools can expect that some students, even those who are very young, will be more knowledgeable about certain technologies than their teachers. While some might decry that situation, it could have a positive effect as teachers and students become even closer partners in learning.

An issue yet to be resolved is the possibility that students with the most technology resources in their home and school may become "technology rich," while those with the least will become "technology poor." A technology study released by the American Association of School Administrators and The

A LEADING FORECASTER PREDICTS/RECOMMENDS

"In the future, schools will be seen as virtual wired centers of learning, not as edifice complexes," concludes Marvin Cetron, president of Forecasting International.

He adds, "As we move into the 21st century, only about half of our students go on to college. Many of the others go into technical fields. We face a shortage of computer programmers, medical technicians, robot technicians, and other specialists. The answer may be found in high-tech vocational training that few school systems can now provide."

Lightspan Partnership in 1998 indicates that 80 percent of educators have seen evidence that technology is improving student achievement and 95 percent say it is particularly helpful in educating low-performing students. On the other hand, students from poorer families are less likely to have advanced technologies in their homes, not for lack of desire, but for lack of resources. Schools and communities must wrestle with how to make technology available to all students at home and at school.

- **Technology is used to increase efficiency and effectiveness in the learning process.**

As we take steps into the new century, many school systems are taking great strides in using technology as a tool for instruction, for benchmarking progress, and for enhancing formal assessment. That trend is likely to continue.

The promise of technology is great, but because technology offers us a new way to store and retrieve information, we must be aware of the pitfalls as well as the benefits. As a new publishing medium, it has not been fully vetted. The conventions we have established that include editorial boards, verification of facts, selection/review committees, copyright, and many other things common to the world of print are not yet established in technology. Therefore, one of the immediate challenges is how to teach learners to be wise and effective users of information. As a result, media literacy courses and units are becoming more commonplace as we approach the 21st century.

- **School systems use technology to enhance planning, simulate possible changes, develop schedules, keep records, ensure accountability, and enhance other functions.**

Technology-based management, record keeping, planning, scheduling, and accountability tools are currently being used, with varying levels of sophistication, in most school systems. From budgets to bus schedules to menu planning, technology has become an invaluable tool.

In some cases, service agencies provide centralized technology services, ranging from record keeping to maintenance of electronic equipment, generally for small or medium-sized school systems. Regional databases are helping teachers and administrators share information, and e-mail is stimulating more frequent conversation. According to Sandra Hamburg of the Committee for Economic Development, "The workplace often restructures as a response to technology and the way it changes the relationships within the working environment."

- **Technology is used in schools to expand the nature and boundaries of knowledge.**

The private and public colleges and universities in the state of North Carolina have joined together in connecting their libraries because no single library can keep up with the new flow of information. Similarly, public school systems that join digital libraries can have at their students' and teachers' fingertips the Library of Congress, the great museums of the world, and thousands of daily bits and pieces of fresh data.

Katie Mulholland, assistant superintendent in Naperville, Ill., provides this reminder—"Information does not become knowledge until it is put to use."

- **All children are engaged in continuous self-learning and know how to access information sources without the immediate help of teachers.**

The combination of information resources in homes and classrooms means that learners will be able to access information in a self-directed manner. For example, the NASA Classroom of the Future conducted a summer workshop for a group of children in grades K-3. One 5-year-old had already established his own home page and tutored a 2nd grader in the creation of her home page. The 2nd grader did not have a computer at home, so the kids and teachers found a business partner that donated a used computer to her family.

"This type of self-learning is an important life skill that many kids may not fully develop if we spoon-feed them," cautions Callie Langohr, a guidance counselor at Flathead High School in Kalispell, Mont.

> *A most important aspect of learning technology is to provide adequate support for teachers to learn and keep abreast of technology developments.*
>
> Harold Howe
> Former U.S. Commissioner of Education
> and Harvard Professor

- **Teachers must have minimum competency requirements in technology for recertification and give evidence of its integrated use in classrooms.**

In identifying this characteristic, the Council of 21 challenges both those who prepare teachers and those who certify them to make sure what they are doing is relevant for educators of the next century.

Kay Toliver, a teacher at P.S. 72, East Harlem Middle School, and star of PBS television programs such as "Good Morning Miss Toliver" and "The Eddie Files," reminds us that technology should not be thought of as just computers. Cameras, camcorders, VCRs, televisions, telephones, calculators, and even the kitchen stove are all technologies in teachers' and students' lives.

Margaret Honey, a researcher at the Educational Development Center, found that it took teachers three years before they were comfortable integrating contemporary technology into the day-to-day activities of the classroom.

That's why the availability of hardware, appropriate software, and adequate training is critical.

Early in the 21st century, the teacher's desk might resemble a console that can be used to call up information and ideas from around the world using many technologies. The benefits of access to and creative use of these resources is another reason why professional development for teachers and administrators is vital.

- **Technology opens the door to self-directed learning.**

Stephen Heyneman, who served for many years as chief of human resources and social policy for The World Bank, tells us that the key to technology use is portability. For example, books, walkmen, and newspapers are portable. So are beepers and cell phones. No student, rich or poor, rural or urban, should be without technological access to information—at home, at school, on the bus, in the library, or anywhere.

Former astronaut George Nelson, director of Project 2061 at the American Association for the Advancement of Science, cautions us about the speed of change. He says the world of technology is moving so fast that, before the ink is dry, some parts of this publication may be outdated.

And as management guru Peter Drucker points out, what the world of work needs is learners not just knowers. Learners are self-directed. They are capable of accessing new information and assimilating it into new and more flexible constructs.

- **Distance learning is extensively used to deliver inservice staff development.**

"Distance learning will be used even more extensively in the 21st century to deliver professional development," Nelson predicts. Indeed, certain educational opportunities will no longer require that you come to them. They will come to you. Whether it is used for the delivery of professional development for adults or to offer learning experiences for students, distance learning should use proven media and supplemental materials.

From the early research on mainframe computer programs such as control Data's Plato System and those developed by IBM, research studies have demonstrated that technology used wisely can increase learning. Studies show that the same content can be mastered in a shorter time and retention is greater with computer-assisted instruction than in traditional lecture classrooms. However, the critical factor is the design of the content software.

Researcher Dexter Fletcher examined distance learning in the military, in all forms, from one-way video teleconference to two-way staff development, and found that it was often as effective if not more effective than face-to-face lectures. From broadcast, recorded, or netcourses, distance learning staff development will be a reality in the 21st century.

Conclusions

On the cusp of a new century, some thoughtful educators are expressing concern about making massive investments in technology at the expense of everything else, even the training needed for effective use of that technology. As reflected in this study, technology is not the answer to school reform, but it is an integral component of the emerging global knowledge/information age. It is a new way of storing and retrieving information. However, more information without the ability to examine and make critical decisions about it is of little help. True progress will be made when people are prepared to find information, work in teams, analyze the information, make decisions, defend those decisions, and take actions.

Additional Characteristics: Contemporary Technology

Other characteristics in this category identified by the Council of 21 include: as in the workplace, technology is used to restructure the education system; the limits of technology are recognized; technology may not be the best teacher of ethics and morals; schools welcome powerful media that provide information that challenges teachers to stay even more current; all students have access at least 2 hours a day, 365 days a year to computer-dependent curriculum packages directly from their homes; each student has a laptop computer; joint curriculum development is conducted by state and federal government agencies and the media/software industry; technology is deployed as learning appliances connected to broadband networks and care is taken to choose the proper types and variety of technology, for example, a personal voice communication device might be more appropriate than a laptop by 2003.

ntegrated/Dynamic/ Competency-Based Curriculum

- Curriculum is linked to clear, challenging standards that are understood by teachers, parents, and students.
- Curriculum is linked to meaningful demonstrations of mastery of knowledge and skills.
- Education is grounded in a "curriculum for life," engaging students in addressing real-world problems, issues important to humanity, and questions that matter.
- Schoolwork is project-based, collaborative, and meaningful.
- School systems incorporate technology in offering productive learning experiences for students.
- Diverse classes and multiple ways of teaching are offered to suit all students.
- Students develop the ability to work cooperatively as members of a team.
- Developmentally appropriate pre-kindergarten programs are commonplace.
- Lesson plans exhibit both an integrated curriculum and attention to multiple intelligences.
- Innovation, creativity, and life-long enjoyment are fostered through the integration of the performing and visual arts, including fine arts and music.
- Students learn about different cultures.
- Students are prepared to live and work within the framework of an information/ knowledge-based society.

The role of education is not only to teach students to earn a living, but to teach them to make a life.

Terry Dozier, U.S. Department of Education
Former National Teacher of the Year

Everyone, including the student, must expect the best.

Grace Williams
Florida Teacher of the Year

We know who our high school graduates will be in the year 2010. They are already in school. How well they are prepared for the world they will inherit and ultimately shape will depend, in large part, on the strength of what we teach them today.

Like many other attributes of the 21st century school, the curriculum cannot be static. While certain bodies of knowledge and skills will remain bedrock, what we teach and how we teach it must include knowledge, skills, and behaviors that reflect our ever-changing society. In many ways, our schools help to shape society. However, they must also be flexible enough to adapt to changes in society, to new ideas, and to the virtual explosion of technology development.

Noted demographer Harold Hodgkinson, a member of the Council of 21, has alerted the nation about the need to adjust to rapidly rising enrollments and the effects of immigration, poverty, and fertility rates on our schools and school systems. While schools address the outcomes of learning, they must also adapt to students who will start at different places or progress at different rates because of social, economic, health, and other conditions in their lives.

The following characteristics of 21st century schools and school systems related to integrated/dynamic/competency-based curriculum were identified by the Council of 21:

- **Curriculum is linked to clear, challenging standards that are understood by teachers, parents, and students.**

As the nation enters a new millennium and as international competition becomes even more heated, many people are calling for (new, higher, better) standards in education. In fact, the 1990s might very well become known as the decade of standards. Many curriculum and other leadership organizations, as well as state departments of education, have answered the call.

Thoughtful critics caution that the process of developing dynamic standards should involve educators and members of the community because collective wisdom is needed if the standards are to have any meaning or gain support. Others warn that standards should not be allowed to freeze the education system in a fast-changing world.

- **Curriculum is linked to meaningful demonstrations of mastery of knowledge and skills.**

Performance-based assessments, sometimes called "authentic assessments," are taking precedence over traditional, standardized, norm-referenced tests. Education consultant William Spady, president of Breakthrough Systems in Dillon, Colo., has called for a movement from time-based to results-based education. When charting outcomes, Spady contends that simply dividing up today's lesson and testing pieces of it might be helpful if done properly, but a longer view is also needed, an assurance that the education students are receiving is actually preparing them for life.

- **Education is grounded in a "curriculum for life," engaging students in addressing real-world problems, issues important to humanity, and questions that matter.**

"Students definitely need to learn what is going on in the world today," says Langohr. "Many kids graduate and know very little about the world [they're part of]."

"If we can't make it real, students may not remember it," adds Florida teacher Grace Williams.

Charlotte-Mecklenberg, N.C., Superintendent Eric Smith encourages educators to consider "a problem-based learning mode" as they prepare students for the new century.

An education for life in the 21st century will require skills in problem solving—not only the ability to address challenges, whatever they turn out to be, but to anticipate the effects of our actions. "In providing a curriculum for life, all of us will need to develop a high comfort level for students to discuss controversial issues," says Gary Rowe, president of Rowe, Inc., in Atlanta.

- **Schoolwork is project-based, collaborative, and meaningful.**

While members of the Council of 21 generally agree that a project-based approach to teaching and learning can be helpful, some express caution. Both Illinois administrator Katie Mulholland, and John Rinaldi, an assistant superintendent in Hinesburg, Vermont., say "project-based" should be further defined. The project should be "meaningful," they say, and should stimulate collaboration and lead to processes that result in a product. "Learning to work with others to accomplish a purpose is a very important life skill," Langohr adds.

- **School systems incorporate technology in offering productive learning experiences for students.**

MIT's Nicholas Negroponte (1995), in his bestseller *Being Digital*, warns that the new technologies and our access to information are growing exponentially. The change is so rapid, according to Marvin Cetron, president for Forecasting International and a member of the Council of 21, that one-fourth of what college engineering students learn in their first year of college is obsolete by graduation. He adds, "Firms with more than 300 employees see education and training as an investment, while firms of under 200 see it as an expense."

Schools in the 21st century must make high tech tools available to students and provide training for teachers in how to use these tools. Most students will likely come to school toting their own personal communications devices. Students whose families are unable or unwilling to provide these devices may find learning more and more difficult if they lack learning tools available to their peers. And unless we head off the problem, we could end up with a split generation of people who are "technology rich" and "technology poor."

- **Diverse classes and multiple ways of teaching are offered to suit all students.**

David Kolb, a professor at Case Western University whose ideas became the basis for the 4MAT system developed by consultant Bernice McCarthy, identifies four styles of learners: imaginative learners, analytic learners, commonsense learners, and dynamic learners. Some students are more attuned to visual and others to oral presentations (Hoyle, English, and Steffy 1998). Further, in our increasingly diverse society, immigrant students, who come to school immersed in another culture and whose first language is other than

English, may also require special attention. This diversity demands multiple ways of teaching. And, of course, students who must cope with individual disabilities have long required special attention. As a result, some schools and school systems are considering the possible benefits and problems associated with developing individualized education plans for all students.

> Growing numbers of students, as we move into the 21st century, are getting information in jolts through television and video games. They are bombarded with fast zooms, tilts, close-ups, long-shots, and flashes of color, with little time to concentrate. A challenge to schools in the new century will be to capture the imaginations of students whose attention spans have often dropped to seconds.

- **Students develop the ability to work cooperatively as members of a team.**

  The need to be able to work with others is emphasized in nearly every category of this study. *Preparing Students for the 21 Century,* an earlier study published by the American Association of School Administrators, states:
  "People, organizations, parts of organizations, and even nations, are interdependent. The ability of people to combine their knowledge and talents to achieve an even higher purpose is synergistic and will be essential to life in the 21st century."

  In businesses and other organizations, more and more people are working in teams that combine employees from a variety of areas to achieve a common goal. Schools and school systems in the 21st century must use even more team management, involving diverse groups of staff and representatives of the community. Teachers, administrators, and school board members will work with parents and others to gain their expertise and to ultimately enrich education. Students will work in teams—some within their school; some within the broader community; and some with people from around the world through the use of technology.

- **Developmentally appropriate pre-kindergarten programs are commonplace.**

  Research has demonstrated that children as young as two years of age have skills that allow them to identify visual symbols such as letters. By the time children enter kindergarten, they have often developed a speaking vocabulary of 2,500 words. As researchers continue to study brain growth and child development, they are revealing a host of challenging conclusions that have educators asking an increasing number of questions, including: Are young children often capable of more than we expect? If we expect too much, will we push the child into a spiral of failure? Should literacy be the main focus of early childhood education programs, or should the focus be on social, emotional, and physical development?

"A child who develops social, emotional, and other skills will likely do better in academics," says Donald Kussmaul, superintendent of schools in East Dubuque, Ill.

Les Omotani, superintendent of the West Des Moines Public Schools in Iowa, agrees, adding, "Rather than a literacy focus, pre-kindergarten programs should have a developmental focus. They should reflect what we've learned from brain research and what we have discovered about the physical, social, and emotional development of children, not just literacy."

"Students are coming to school less and less prepared," adds Mary Ann Sonntag, a principal in Winston-Salem, North Carolina. "We need to help level that playing field in kindergarten."

Researchers tell us that children develop up to 50 percent of their ultimate intelligence by age 5. During these early years, children develop skills that become a foundation for all subsequent education. The challenge for schools is to share what they know about child growth and development with parents and others in the community and to offer or lend their considerable expertise to pre-kindergarten programs.

- **Lesson plans exhibit both an integrated curriculum and attention to multiple intelligences.**

All well-educated persons have mastered certain bodies of knowledge. However, the person who is wise understands the relationships, the connective tissue that unites much of what we know. Harvard professor and scientist Edward O. Wilson argues in his book *Consilience* that there is a fundamental "unity of knowledge," and that a small number of natural laws underlie every branch of learning.

As we head into the 21st century, many schools are already moving in the direction of an integrated curriculum and the teaching of higher-order thinking and reasoning skills. The Council also suggests that schools must better understand what another Harvard professor, Howard Gardner, has described as "multiple intelligences." Gardner suggests that there are many forms of intelligence, including linguistic, logical, musical, spatial, bodily/kinesthetic, interpersonal, and intrapersonal, and that people possess different combinations and levels of these intelligences.

- **Innovation, creativity, and lifelong enjoyment are fostered through integration of the performing and visual arts, including fine arts and music.**

While the arts are a discipline in themselves, they also represent basic forms of communication and lead to connections with and among other parts of the curriculum. Some questions we might ask about the arts are: How is it possible to study history without examining the arts? And how can students understand music, writing, visual images, dance, design, architecture, even the handiwork of nature, without an appreciation of the arts?

The Council of 21 also points out that a grounding in the arts leads to innovation, lifelong enjoyment, and creative thinking, all of which are important. Indeed, Johns Hopkins Professor Arnold Packer, who produced the celebrated SCANS report on workforce readiness, declares that the creativity of our people is one of the greatest strengths of our country's 21st century workforce.

When students are engaged in the arts, they develop a broader understanding of the interrelated aspects of the world. Throughout history, the arts have been at the forefront of attempts to raise and clarify the issues of humanity and the needs of society. Schools for the 21st century must help students discover their ability to express themselves and to be creative. Those students will ultimately apply the knowledge and skills learned through the arts in every other aspect of their lives.

- **Students learn about different cultures.**

We must understand the cultures of the world if we hope to understand our own country. Schools and school systems in the 21st century must make adjustments to allow for the changing pluralism of America while preparing students to live, work, and serve in a diverse society.

- **Students are prepared to live and work within the framework of an information/knowledge-based society.**

Members of the Council of 21 urge that the use of new technologies be integrated into a comprehensive curriculum. The benefits of being able to use technology go far beyond the preparation for a career or avocation.

Heyneman suggests that as we move into the future "there will be few distinctions among the types of occupational demands for which students are preparing." Getting ready for a specific vocation, he says, may be less important than having those skills, habits, and bodies of knowledge that are basic to most, if not all, personal and professional endeavors.

The Council of 21 suggests that business and professional people be involved in curriculum decisions that affect employability.

ADDITIONAL CHARACTERISTICS: INTEGRATED/DYNAMIC/ COMPETENCY-BASED CURRICULUM:

The Council of 21 identified a few additional characteristics of 21st Century schools and school systems related to curriculum. These include the presence of vocational education that supports the infrastructure of an information-based society and the inclusion of business in curriculum decisions affecting vocational programs.

CHAPTER 4

A Focus on Student Performance

- Students possess an expanding number of foundation skills, including, but not limited to, skills in reading, writing, and mathematics.

- Schools expect development of critical thinking and other higher level skills, such as learning to learn.

- Students are capable of thinking creatively in such subjects as literature, the arts, culture, history, geography, science, communications skills, and mathematics.

- The education system promotes the human values inherent in a democracy, including honesty, respect, trustworthiness, caring, and responsibility.

- Students emerge as civil, responsible citizens.

- Students develop a love of learning.

- Schools and society produce lifelong learners with the characteristics necessary for success in life, such as perseverance and curiosity.

- Students develop practical skills important in everyday life.

- Passion and joy for the curriculum is enhanced by making connections across disciplines.

Expectations that students will perform at increasingly high levels will continue long past the turning of a new century, the Council of 21 predicts.

"Most of what we've identified in this category is expected today," remarks Joseph Aguerrebere, deputy director, education, knowledge, and religion at the Ford Foundation.

"A focus on student learning is central to this entire study," says Dorothy Rich, president of the Home and School Institute. "It's the reason all of the other categories in this study exist."

The following characteristics related to a focus on student performance in schools and school systems for the 21st century were identified by the Council 21:

- **Students possess an expanding number of foundation skills, including, but not limited to, skills in reading, writing, and mathematics.**

Education reformers have consistently believed certain core skills must be learned by all students. While the list of "fundamentals" continues to grow, most agree that skills in reading, writing, and math are essential.

Sue Walters, a teacher from Wells Junior High School in Kennebunk, Maine, contends that reading, writing, and math are needed for continued learning and should not be lost in our race toward the future.

Gary Rowe believes that for people to be truly literate in the 21st century, they must be able to communicate and operate within a worldwide framework.

Technology, he says, is making the world's intellectual resources instantly available. Without the ability to access, understand, and use [technology], a person might be seen as less than literate in the global knowledge/information age.

- **Schools expect development of critical thinking and other higher level skills, such as learning to learn.**

Critical thinking and higher level skills "should be thoroughly integrated into all content areas," according to Harold Brewer, superintendent of the Montgomery County School District in Troy, North Carolina. The ability to observe, collect, analyze, and make decisions based on data will be essential in the 21st century. Superintendent Cornelius Cain of the Camp Hill School District in Camp Hill, Pennsylvania, believes that the ability to use critical thinking and decision-making skills "may be one of the most important outcomes of the educational process."

Students should be taught to continue to learn outside the formal school day, to think about what they've learned, and to apply what they've learned in their own lives whether a teacher is present or not. "We need to help students become resourceful," suggests Thomas Fegley, superintendent of schools in Collinsville, Illinois.

Floretta McKenzie, president of the McKenzie Group and a former Washington, D.C., school superintendent, declares that critical thinking and decision-making skills deserve "high priority."

Huong Tran Nguyen, a Long Beach, Calif., educator and a former Disney Teacher of the Year, offers a reminder that "teachers need to be trained in how to develop these skills in their students."

- **Students are capable of thinking creatively in such subjects as literature, the arts, culture, history, geography, science, communications skills, and mathematics.**

This study makes it clear that students will need not only to understand and have skills related to such bodies of knowledge as literature, the arts, culture, history, geography, science, communications, and mathematics, but must also develop the ability to think about and make solid use of this knowledge in their daily lives.

TIME TO THINK

The amount of time that a teacher allows between the completion of a question and the student response influences student performance. By waiting the necessary three to five seconds for the student to begin the response, the teacher can: (1) increase the length of the response, (2) receive more solicited responses, and (3) improve student confidence.

Source: M. Rowe, "Wait-Time and Rewards as Instructional Variables..." *Journal of Research on Science Teaching,* February 1974.

Terry Dozier, a former National Teacher of the Year who currently serves as special adviser to the U.S. Secretary of Education, reminds us that "studies such as this one should reflect all of the world's cultures and their contributions to civilization."

Superintendent Barbara Rommel of the David Douglas School District #40, in Portland, Oregon, says students should be able to integrate and think critically across many subjects, that they should see subjects as not necessarily separate but as part of a larger whole.

Members of the Council of 21 call for a definition of "well prepared." Philippe Lemaitre, corporate vice president and chief technology officer for AMP Inc., urges educators to consider "understanding, application, and creative thinking as part of that definition."

NATIONAL GOALS FOR EDUCATION

Goals 2000: The Educate America Act, adopted by the U.S. Congress, includes eight goals for American education, to be realized by the year 2000. They are:

- All children will start school ready to learn.

- The high school graduation rate will increase to at least 90 percent.

- All students will leave grades 4, 8, and 12 having demonstrated competency over challenging subject matter, including English, mathematics, science, foreign languages, civics and government, economics, arts, history, and geography.

- Every school will ensure that all students learn to use their minds well, so they are prepared for responsible citizenship, further learning, and productive employment in our nation's modern economy.

- The nation's students will be first in the world in mathematics and science achievement.

- Every adult will be literate and possess the knowledge and skills necessary to compete in a global economy and exercise the rights and responsibilities of citizenship.

- Every school will be free of drugs, violence, firearms, and alcohol and will offer a disciplined environment conducive to learning.

- Teachers will have access to programs to improve their professional skills and acquire the knowledge and skills necessary to instruct and prepare all students for the next century.

- Every school will promote partnerships to increase parental involvement and participation in promoting the social, emotional, and academic growth of children.

- **The education system promotes the human values inherent in a democracy, including honesty, respect, trustworthiness, caring, and responsibility.**

Our quality of life depends on much more than just our ability to earn a living. Most would agree that a healthy family life and the willingness to contribute to the community are basic building blocks of a civil society. According to Kay Toliver, "Education must prepare students to make it in life. Skills they acquire must enable them to have and use common sense as well as their book smarts."

In the past, some groups have openly criticized schools for teaching values, while educators asserted that a value-free education is not possible. Today, the demand is growing for schools to teach certain values basic to sustaining a free and democratic society and to maintaining our domestic tranquility. *Preparing Students for the 21st Century* revealed a demand for education that would help students develop a sense of civic virtue, engage in ethical behavior, understand and apply conflict resolution techniques, take responsibility for their own actions, and understand the effects of their actions on others.

- **Students emerge as civil, responsible citizens.**

"Education should help us sustain our democratic society," says Monica Bradsher. "It is one of the main justifications for a tax-supported system of public education."

American scholar R. Freeman Butts describes values he believed to be "the obligations of citizenship." Those values or obligations include: justice, equality, truth, authority, participation, patriotism, diversity, privacy, freedom, due process, human rights, and property.

Some of the demand in this area is being driven by breaches in ethical behavior and violence that seems to pervade society. Civic education, including law-related education, can help students build an even more civil society in the 21st century. The Center for Civic Education in Calabasas, California, has developed a framework for civic education, which is being used as a basis for strengthening democracy in many parts of the world. Not only do students learn to become better citizens through CIVITAS, they also learn to apply their thinking skills as they discuss topics such as "unity vs. diversity," "liberty vs. order," and a host of other issues basic to a democracy.

The CIVITAS framework has three components: civic virtue, civic participation, and civic knowledge. The program helps students develop qualities such as: civility, individual responsibility, self-discipline, civic-mindedness, open-mindedness, compromise, understanding of diversity, patience and persistence, compassion, generosity, and loyalty to the nation and its principles.

- **Students develop a love of learning.**

It is the nature of infants and children, left on their own, to engage in pleasurable things. Why shouldn't a love of learning be one of them? While no class can reflect the exciting totality of human existence, it can reflect excitement, adventure, and beauty.

The challenge in an information-rich world is to organize countless resources in a way that will be engaging, challenging, and motivating for young learners. Rowe reminds us that when students become engaged in accomplishing an academic task and receive appropriate recognition for it, they develop a love of learning.

- **Schools and society produce lifelong learners with the characteristics necessary for success in life, such as perseverance and curiosity.**

The person who is curious and who perseveres will very likely be well educated throughout life.

As stated earlier, Drucker has said that what the workforce needs is learners and not knowers. The workforce needs people who have the abilities, skills, and knowledge that enable them to work together in teams to accomplish tasks. This means individuals must have the perseverance to complete a task no matter how hard. Moreover, they must have the curiosity that leads them to new ways of solving old problems and engages their imaginations. Philipe Lemaitre declares that perseverance and curiosity should be coupled with enthusiasm.

The learners of the future must be flexible, lifelong learners. According to Wadi Haddad, president of Knowledge Enterprise, "The idea that knowledge is fixed, finite, and bounded is a convention of the world of books and is incomplete. Knowledge communicated as image, sound, graphical representation, and text in electronic form changes this idea. Knowledge is a dynamic, changeable, interactive process and extendable."

As we move into a new century, students will need to deal with as yet unimagined problems and opportunities that will require their very best thinking and effort. They will need to maintain a high level of flexibility and creative thinking and to persevere.

Tugging against some students who are potentially strong performers is a tendency to turn those who achieve into outcasts. Schools must deal with this perennial problem, which could cost our nation the fully developed talents of legions of future workers and citizens.

- **Students develop practical skills important in everyday life.**

The United States Department of Labor for years has been telling us that the average worker will change jobs at least five times during his work life. This may not simply be a shift in employer, but a dramatic change in the type and scope of work.

Members of the Council of 21 note that, as life has become more complicated, many college graduates are lacking what would generally be considered practical skills, such as preparing income tax forms, repairing a faucet, changing a tire, or managing personal finances. Schools of the 21st century will be asked to remedy this situation.

- **Passion and joy for the curriculum is enhanced by making connections across disciplines.**

The need for seeing connections goes far beyond school to the life students will lead after graduation. Nancy Stover says that "successful workers are multi-functional and interdisciplinary in their approach to all group-related efforts as well as in their pursuit of professional development." The ability to see connections may indeed be the mark of a truly educated and wise person.

"We need to somehow diminish the territorial boundaries between disciplines, both in conceptual development and in the structure of school facilities," explains Bradsher.

Some members of the Council of 21 note that "passion and joy" may be hard to measure, but generally agree that an integrated curriculum bolsters these characteristics in schools and is essential to preparing students for a global knowledge/information age.

ADDITIONAL CHARACTERISTICS: A FOCUS ON STUDENT PERFORMANCE

The Council of 21 also identified and considered the following characteristics of schools and school systems for the 21st century: students emerge media/information literate; students learn to maintain health throughout life, including nutrition, exercise, and how to evaluate and obtain healthcare; students understand the relationship between what they learn and their potential professional lives; all students master a language other than their own; students are proficient speakers who communicate effectively; and the operation of schools exemplifies the characteristics of a democratic society.

CHAPTER 5

Student-Centered Systems

- All students are valued and provided the individual resources they need to succeed.
- The primary focus of teaching and learning is the student.
- Curriculum is flexible, student-focused, and purposefully designed to help students achieve.
- Students, teachers, parents, and other caregivers work together to address development of the whole child.
- Low-income students have as many advantages in schools as wealthy students.
- Every student is treated with respect.
- High expectations exist for all students.
- Learning experiences challenge students to grow and improve.
- Each school focuses on the needs of its customers—children and parents, first and foremost—along with society at large.
- All students have equal access to technology resources.

"All around us we see evidence that we are in the midst of a cultural transformation, fueled by the recognition that the competition, independence, and isolation of the past cannot elevate the capacities of the human spirit that will energize and guide us in the next phase of our development as we create new ways of being together in the world. Human interdependence, not independence, will be the foundation for a new global civilization, one that will require new mental models and structures for learning."

Stephanie Pace Marshall
President, Illinois Math
and Science Academy

Thoughtful critics of our education system frequently express concern that schools work so hard to satisfy the needs of adults that they have too little time and energy left for students. Schools and systems are faced with everything from political mandates to parent and staff needs to amusement parks that lobby to keep schools from opening before Labor Day so their student employees can stay on the job until the parks close for the season.

Many of these time-consuming pressures and demands are legitimate. However, schools and school systems in the 21st century, while considering and being sensitive to adult needs, must become more student-centered.

The following characteristics of student-centered schools and schools systems for the 21st century were identified by the Council of 21:

- **All students are valued and provided the individual resources they need to succeed.**

The Council of 21 emphasizes that the operative word here is "all." Our concept of work in a global knowledge/information age is changing. There are fewer unskilled jobs, and the digital age is replacing some workers because of the efficiency of technology. For example, 30 years ago, *The New York Times* had 4,000 Linotype operators; today, 50 computer composers have replaced them.

"We can't afford to write off anyone, since there are simply not enough unskilled jobs to take up the slack for those who fall through the cracks," says Monica Bradsher.

"One of the best ways for us to value our students and help them succeed is to have high expectations for them," adds Fairfax County, Va., teacher Kimberly Cetron.

Callie Langohr cautions that "schools need to give students a fair chance, but what they do with it is their choice."

Schools capable of preparing students for life in the new century must provide the material tools and human resources needed to help every child reach his or her potential. However, schools will not be able to do the job alone. Learners will need to be able to access information and support from their homes, libraries, and community centers. Working together, schools and the communities they serve must make education and the success of students a top priority. Their success will take many forms—individual success, contributions to society, and excellence in the workplace.

- **The primary focus of teaching and learning is the student.**

During the 20th century, most schools in the United States adhered to an industrial model, which placed the teacher in control of instruction. The system itself took on some of the characteristics of an assembly line. Children were placed in school at around six years of age. After 12 years, we assumed they would come out well educated. Until shortly after World War II, system dropouts or rejects of the assembly line model left school to find employment in the unskilled labor market.

As we move into the 21st century, students face a more competitive world with fewer unskilled jobs. The worldwide economy is demanding more cognitive workers who possess a high level of creativity. Whether in the workplace or as citizens, people in the new century will have to become more self-directed.

To adjust to these changing needs, schools have for the last quarter of the 20th century been exploring new and different paradigms for education. Significantly, they have shifted from teacher-centered to student-centered programs. In the 21st century, teachers, who must themselves continue to learn, will face students who have access to information from all over the world. Therefore, teachers will become orchestrators of learning, helping students turn information into knowledge and knowledge into wisdom. "Too often, adults dictate the classes kids will take and make decisions with little or no student feedback," Langohr observes. "That is inconsistent with putting students at the center of our work."

William Spady emphasizes that time spent on the education assembly line has too thoroughly defined a student's school career—a year of English, four years of math. What is crucial, Spady says, is that students achieve important outcomes that enable them to be successful in life.

- **Curriculum is flexible, student-focused, and purposefully designed to help students achieve.**

Some have criticized American education for promoting breadth over depth of learning. While the curriculum must be flexible, student-focused, and purposeful, it must go even further. Simply making it possible for students to explore is not enough. Schools will need to help students develop a discipline for learning. "Flexibility is fine, but we still must have some continuity, some scope and sequence," says Marilyn Mathis, superintendent in Murfreesboro, Tennessee.

"Student achievement should reflect not only student desires but also the needs of society, perhaps reflected in community-based standards," suggests Mulholland.

Fundamentals will not disappear in the 21st century. However, the teaching of them must become more flexible and personal, taking into account the interests and desires of each student.

- **Students, teachers, parents, and other caregivers work together to address development of the whole child.**

When students enter school, they often reflect the advantages and disadvantages of the community in which they were reared. When parents devote themselves to bringing out the best in their children, many disadvantages fade.

Educating a child takes teamwork. Schools need the help and support of parents and the community. The close of the 20th century finds more than 75 percent of children under age 18 with parents working outside the home because of economic necessity and the desire to pursue a career. Therefore, childcare providers also play an important role in getting children ready for school.

Some schools, as part of parent-teacher conferences, work with parents to develop a teacher-parent plan of action. The teacher, parent, or other caregiver, and sometimes the student, agree on what each should do to help ensure the student's success in school.

- **Low-income students have as many advantages in schools as wealthy students.**

While a response to this challenge is yet to be fully developed, educators and school systems across the nation are focusing on equal opportunity for all students, whatever their backgrounds. Some have eliminated tracking. Others are working to make technology as equally available as possible to all students. Most are fighting for the financial support they need to sustain their efforts.

"No student should ever be disadvantaged by what the school does or does not do," says Harold Brewer. "Some students will always come to school more advantaged because of the extra support available in their homes."

Former U.S. Commissioner of Education, superintendent, and Harvard professor Harold "Doc" Howe II declares this issue one of the most important schools face as we move into the 21st century.

- **Every student is treated with respect.**

Children as well as adults respond to recognition and appreciation. The school is one place where everyone should be treated with respect. Stephen Heyneman notes that not only should students feel a sense of respect, but they should also demonstrate a respect for others. This sense of respect should permeate the entire school, from the lunchroom and boiler room to the classroom, superintendent's office, and board room.

In summing up Council of 21 deliberations at historic Mount Vernon, then AASA President Karl Hertz declared that one true goal of this millennial project is "liberating the genius of our children…and teaching them to be good people."

- **High expectations exist for all students.**

We rise to our expectations. If we envision ourselves as successful in various ways, our chances of reaching our dreams improve immensely. Without such expectations, we lack direction or a star to guide us. Not only should schools and school systems for the 21st century have high expectations for their students, but their communities should have high expectations for their schools. Those expectations should be accompanied by the support needed to help students and schools achieve. After all, an expectation or standard unaccompanied by the necessary resources becomes nothing more than a form of punishment.

- **Learning experiences challenge students to grow and improve.**

Sophie Sa, executive director of the Panasonic Foundation, cautions us not to limit students because we feel they cannot realistically accomplish something. While adults may sometimes feel a learning experience is beyond a student's ability, we should err on the side of giving the child encouragement and the tools to be successful.

Brewer cautions that when parents resist higher expectations simply to hold their children back, the community needs to intervene on behalf of all students. All students should be encouraged to undertake a wide range of learning experiences, from those found in the school curriculum to those in the community, from exploring learning opportunities available through technology to pursuing creative ideas.

- **Each school focuses on the needs of its customers— children and parents, first and foremost—along with society at large.**

While most educators agree that students are the primary "clients" of our schools, others believe that American society, including parents, comes in at least a close second. If we hope to maintain our free and democratic society and free-market economy, we must invest in the education of our children. "Children, parents, and community all benefit from our education system," adds George Nelson.

- **All students have equal access to technology resources.**

Gordon Ambach, executive director of the Council of Chief State School Officers, in testifying before the Federal Communications Commission, stated that until computers are as ubiquitous as books, pens, and tablets, there will be no equity. Moreover, true equity will not exist until every student has access to technology both in and out of school.

As we near the turn of the century, AASA, in collaboration with The Lightspan Partnership, released a study indicating that investments in software and teacher training need to accompany purchases or leasing of hardware. At the news conference releasing results of this study, AASA Executive Director Paul Houston stated that, "The good news is that educators attributed a significant increase in student achievement to technology. The bad news is the digital divide is widening between students who have access to computers at home and those who don't."

ADDITIONAL CHARACTERISTICS: STUDENT-CENTERED SYSTEMS

In addressing student-centered Systems, the Council of 21 identified nearly 20 additional characteristics of schools and school systems capable of preparing students for a global knowledge/information age, many of which are similar to other items discussed in this chapter. They include: learning is meaningful and useful in children's lives; individual learning styles and abilities are recognized and addressed; students work and think while teachers facilitate the learning process; key values are fostered in the education process, such as enthusiasm for knowledge building, discipline, logic, and hard work; instructional processes cultivate informed, self-directed competence building; schools engage students in the democratic process to help them learn to become active, responsible citizens; students learn in an environment that allows for risk and promotes conflict resolution and problem solving; each child is met at his or her own level; students are expected to have high aspirations; education liberates the genius and goodness of all children; students with limited community/family support are empowered; every student has a personal adult advocate; students who can achieve above the norm are encouraged and given the opportunity to do so; education is about inspiration and aspiration, not uncritical self-esteem; developmentally appropriate learning experiences are provided for young children; student ideas and voices are considered when planning curriculum and school procedures; programs are based, to some extent, on the needs/potentials of students currently enrolled; heterogeneous grouping is used to enhance all student learning; and schools observe the success of students 10 years after they graduate.

road Academic and Social Context

- Learning extends beyond the walls of schools, facilities, and specific disciplines.
- There is a global focus, building on the strength of our diversity and our shared culture and values.
- Technology enhances the learning process for all students.
- All learners view themselves as part of the learning community.
- The system emphasizes respect for other persons and ideas.
- There is a re-emphasis on democracy that values change, dissent, variety, and talents for learning, including intelligence beyond books.
- Parents assist and guide their children's education.
- Students learn conflict-resolution, communications, and other skills that enable them to collaborate within a diverse group.
- Technology is used to provide students rich, multicultural experiences.
- School systems understand and deal with the effects of poverty on learning, family structure, and students' overall lives.

"It seems to me that teaching can only be satisfactory if it awakens some response in you. More information is no good. It gives you nothing more than what you had before."

Agatha Christie's autobiography 1977

Students have traditionally been asked to master certain skills that allow them to function in society, skills such as listening, speaking, writing, reading, mathematics, and more recently, electronic literacy. In the 21st century, the key elements of education will become more expansive. According to Joseph Aguerrebere, "Students will need to see themselves in an international dimension, since communication seems to have made our world even smaller, and they will need to be able to use technology that will extend their learning far beyond the school site."

The following characteristics of 21st schools and school systems capable of offering a broad academic and social context were identified by the Council of 21:

- **Learning extends beyond the walls of schools, facilities, and specific disciplines.**

Callie Langohr emphasizes that much of learning takes place in the interactions students have with other students, the community, and their parents. In reality, a high school graduate will have spent only about one-ninth of her waking hours in a formal educational setting. Schools compete with many other engaging activities, from Little Leagues to television, for the attention and time of their students.

As we move into the 21st century, educators must ask themselves what it is that engages a student to spend time on sports, musical and other artistic events, science fairs, computer games, or television. It is not that we want formal education to revert to entertainment, but we must be aware of why these and other activities motivate and attract people. Every child is entitled to learning experiences that quicken the spirit of wonder and awaken a quest for knowledge. For example, can we make the study of American history as engaging as other activities open to students? The answer is yes, and some teachers are already doing a masterful job of it.

"We need to think of learning as a process, not as a place," says Omotani, helping to capture the essence of this characteristic.

- **There is a global focus, building on the strength of our diversity and our shared culture and values.**

"With our great diversity, America should think of itself as a kind of United Nations," says Gary Rowe. "Our diversity is or should be a treasured asset."

> The world is both larger and smaller for today's students than it has been in the past. In 1900, the world population reached 1 billion. By the early 21st century, we will have a world population of 6 billion. The average 19-year-old in 1900 had not traveled more than 50 miles from his birthplace. As we move into the 21st century, jet aircraft take us nearly anywhere in the world in a matter of hours. In the digital age, it is possible for any 18-year-old to contact legions of people everywhere on earth through telephone or e-mail communications.

- **Technology enhances the learning process for all students.**

Today's infant is literally surrounded by an ocean of information. By the time children reach school, they will have heard more from broadcast or recorded voice messages than from face-to-face contact. The consensus of the Council of 21, the Council of Advisers, and representatives of gravity-breaking schools and school systems is that digital technology will play a constantly increasing role in education.

In the 21st century, each home will have access to a digital library 24 hours a day, provided people have the proper equipment and can afford to pay their communications bills. They will have more control over information, and will need to be media literate, able to separate truth from propaganda. Some will develop their own web pages. Therefore, schools will be challenged to make the very best use of technology in enhancing education.

- **All learners view themselves as part of the learning community.**

To comfortably survive, every person must become a lifelong learner, according to Vic Klatt, education policy coordinator for the U.S. House Committee on Education and the Workforce. As information and knowledge increase at a spectacular rate, and as our workforce is constantly challenged to adjust to new jobs and new roles, if we don't keep up, we'll be left out.

In a true learning community, everyone is learning, intellectually and emotionally, from everyone else. There is a free flow of ideas and built-in reinforcement and correction. A stimulating learning environment creates a web or network that encourages students, teachers, administrators, parents, and others to share information and ideas. In this type of environment, educators become constructive critics of the system and make continuous improvements. No longer will it be possible to wait for the seven-year evaluation to make needed changes. Educators must instead spend more time improving and updating education and less time defending it.

"Rather than teachers simply passing down information and knowledge, they must be actively engaged in their own learning throughout their careers, and they must work side by side, learning constantly from each other," adds Kimberley Cetron.

"When we speak of learners, we must be speaking of students, teachers, other staff, parents, and community," says Les Omotani.

- **The system emphasizes respect for other persons and ideas.**

When schools embody the principles of a democratic community for students and adults, they foster respect for other persons and ideas. Such schools make it more likely that we will respect rather than reject other people, while honestly questioning new ideas. In some cases, we may even agree to disagree.

Respect must permeate school systems. Parents and the community should demonstrate their respect for education and educators, and educators should demonstrate their respect for students, parents, and the community. Teachers and students should share a mutual respect. A climate of respect, a climate that preserves and builds the dignity of people, serves as a platform for an even more effective system of education for the next century.

- **There is a re-emphasis on democracy that values change, dissent, variety, and talents for learning, including intelligence beyond books.**

In some school systems, educators are teaching about democracy and giving their students experiences in how to live and work in a democratic society. Too often, however, students attend schools that are autocratic, where their ideas about education are neither sought nor valued.

These experiences help students develop intelligence that goes beyond what they study in books. Applying the principles of democracy to the way schools and school systems operate makes education more applicable to real life. If we hope to prepare students for life in a democracy, their school and school system must serve as a microcosm of a democratic society, recommends Kimberley Cetron. In reality, democracy leads to dissent, variety, encouragement of unique talents, and ultimately strength.

- **Parents assist and guide their children's education.**

Schools know they can't do it alone. They need the help and support of parents and the community. Some parents consider their involvement so important that they actually end run the system, withdrawing into an option such as home schooling. While schools certainly can't accept every parental idea, they must increasingly try to pay attention and to learn from parents who are often very well educated and generally capable of being a full partner in their child's education. In the 21st century, parents and educators will become even more of a team, together focused on helping students learn, grow, and prepare for life after graduation.

- **Students learn conflict-resolution, communications, and other skills that enable them to collaborate within a diverse group.**

As the world becomes more populated and as our society becomes more diverse, we need tools to help us live peaceful, fulfilled lives. Harold Hodgkinson illustrated for the Council of 21 how the nation is becoming increasingly diverse by explaining that soon no single group will constitute 50 percent of American society. Everyone will be a minority.

Students who emerge from our schools should be masters at understanding and celebrating differences, identifying and dealing with injustice, finding common ground, exercising diplomatic skills, and practicing the techniques of conflict management.

As we move into the 21st century, communications skills will be survival skills. We must help our students, and ourselves, learn to communicate effectively across cultures and languages and to resolve conflicts productively when they arise.

- **Technology is used to provide students rich, multicultural experiences.**

Nancy Stover believes that technology does, and will to an even greater extent in the future, provide students with rich, multicultural experiences. With digital compression and the vast increase in broadcast, cable, and direct broadcast satellite television channels, plus the instant connections provided by the Internet, expanded multicultural experiences are possible, even inevitable, as students are connected to nearly every part of the world.

Cornelius Cain predicts "technology will revolutionize education, just as it has business and industry." Meanwhile, Michael Sullivan, executive director of the Institute for Instructional Technology, cautions that it takes more than technology to build true intercultural and international understanding.

44

- **School systems understand and deal with the effects of poverty on learning, family structure, and students' overall lives.**

The battle against poverty will continue into the 21st century, and because it has a profound effect on students and their future chances in life, schools must be at the forefront of the battle as advocates for children and youth. Schools and school systems must also adjust to provide students from all economic and social groups an equal opportunity to learn and succeed. Much will depend on policy and how forcefully it is carried out.

ADDITIONAL CHARACTERISTICS: BROAD ACADEMIC AND SOCIAL CONTEXT

The Council of 21 identified a number of other characteristics in this category, some of which are related to those discussed in this chapter. They are: students learn about international trends and are encouraged to see themselves as participants in local, national, and international economics; schools meet the needs of the disabled; students come together at a place called school to participate in a common learning experience for our diverse nation; schools embody the principles of a democratic community for students and adults; schools are not defined as a place, but as a networked community; multicultural understanding imbues the curriculum; the concept of "family" is rekindled; foundational national beliefs and cornerstone elements are strengthened; while experiencing global cultures and values, all students' own roots and national values and beliefs are reinforced; and students come together to learn about the strength of diversity.

CHAPTER 7

Effective Standards and Assessment

- Schools, families, and communities share high expectations for student performance.
- The same high standards exist for all, but the means for reaching them reflect students' needs and priorities.
- Standards and assessment systems are understood and supported by parents and students.
- Learning is not defined by seat time, but by what is actually learned.
- A commitment exists to continuously improve every aspect of the school system's capabilities and performance.
- Assessment of student achievement extends beyond traditional paper-and-pencil tests.
- Students are able to synthesize, assess, and evaluate achievement.
- Administrators set a tone of high expectations.
- No upper limits are placed on learning and achievement.
- Assessment supports the learning process.

Educational excellence for our students can best be achieved when we have total involvement of teachers, students, administrators, and parents to establish and cultivate a dialogue among all parties in setting goals for our schools.

Edward D. DiPrete
Former Governor of Rhode Island
1991

Schools and school systems are increasingly being asked to develop standards leading to success for students. With the pace of change, those standards must be flexible so they do not freeze the system or its students into a past or present that is fleeting.

On the topic of rigorous standards, Gary Rowe asserts that, "Making information in schools subservient to what the teachers know or don't know makes little sense in an information age. It is possible to develop courses and curricula, along with professional practices, that allow for student exploration beyond fixed parameters. Excellent teachers who can operate comfortably in this environment are part of the real worth of a school."

The following characteristics of 21st century schools and school systems that address the need for effective standards and assessment were identified by the Council of 21:

- **Schools, families, and communities share high expectations for student performance.**

As schools and school systems approach the 21st century, many are looking at forecasts, charting demographics, speculating on what students will need to know and be able to do, monitoring brain research, and developing significant vision statements to guide them.

Most people accept the idea that high expectations are essential, if coupled with the resources to help students meet them. Expectations that are thoughtfully developed, in concert with school staff, families, communities, and students themselves are most likely to take hold. After all, it is hard to feel a sense of ownership without some level of involvement.

Expectation-setting should take place at all levels, from the school district to the school building to the classroom. Some expectations may be districtwide; others may be discrete, focused primarily on the special needs of a single student. The expectation-setting process provides an opportunity for educators to not only involve but also to educate the community about how children learn, how they are working on behalf of students, and how the community can help.

- **The same high standards exist for all, but the means for reaching them reflect students' needs and priorities.**

Every thoughtful discussion of standards leads to a concern that simply setting them isn't enough. Schools also need the resources to help all students reach those standards. That could mean the teacher's approach is tailor-made to match a student's learning style. It also could mean working with a student who has suffered from poverty, who comes from an entirely different culture or part of the world, or who has seen or been a victim of traumatic violence. Ruling on standards and realizing them for every student will require a concerted effort and steadfast support from every school system and its community.

Most everyone, at one time or another, has complained about "double standards." That concern, unfortunately, has plagued schools for decades. For example, when a student is placed in a lower track, the curriculum is a bit less rigorous and each day the student gets further behind his or her classmates. In an endeavor as vital as education, convenience for educators and schools must be balanced against potential benefits or losses for children.

- **Standards and assessment systems are understood and supported by parents and students.**

In the 21st century, educators must help their communities understand that we need to change our mindsets about how schools should work. The A, B, C, D, F scoreboard is a product of a society that insists on winners and losers. The nation is finally discovering that we can't simply give grades and give up. Those who fail become costly for all of us.

- **Learning is not defined by seat time, but by what is actually learned.**

William Spady has fought a long and noble battle on behalf of student learning. His argument is that, for years, schools have been time-based while they need to be outcome- or results-based. His bottom line is that simply completing 5 years of school or 10 courses is not as important as what students actually learn and can apply in their lives. In short, learning cannot be defined by seat time.

- **A commitment exists to continuously improve every aspect of the school system's capabilities and performance.**

During the final decade of the 20th century, schools started paying attention to total quality management. Ultimately, after fits and starts, some school systems picked up and ran with continuous improvement, a basic concept underlying TQM.

A case in point is the Pinellas County Public Schools in Florida. Under the leadership of Superintendent J. Howard Hinesley, the school system is driven by a set of compelling goals and a commitment to continuous improvement. Even students track their individual progress and work directly with teachers to figure out how they can improve. State, district, school, classroom, and student goals are all translated into learning experiences and assessed. The core values of the Pinellas County Schools include: customer-driven quality, leadership, continual improvement, employee participation and development, fast response, design quality and prevention, long-range outlook, management by fact, partnership development, organizational responsibility and citizenship, and a results orientation.

"Continuous improvement needs to be institutionalized," says John O'Rourke, superintendent in Pittsford, N.Y., and a former National Superintendent of the Year whose school system won the coveted "Excelsior" quality award. O'Rourke adds, "Continuous improvement means you'll never get there, but you continue to strive for even better education."

- **Assessment of student achievement extends beyond traditional paper-and-pencil tests.**

As we enter the third millennium, many schools are using performance-based assessments. They are building portfolios that contain everything from writing samples to explanations of how a student got the right (or wrong) answer to a math problem.

Multiple-choice and fill-in-the-blank tests are now being supplemented in many school systems by performance-based assessments, which are aimed directly at gauging a student's performance on a day-to-day basis and providing individualized help to the student. These assessments typically include portfolios of student work.

48

- **Students are able to synthesize, assess, and evaluate achievement.**

In Pinellas County, Florida, classroom goals are posted on the wall and students keep a record of their individual goals on their desks. When students complete an assignment, they are eager to have the teacher review it and make suggestions. They want to move on to the next, more challenging assignment, and can almost always explain why what they're learning will be important to them in that next assignment and in their lives.

The picture here is one of engaging students in their own education. It is firing their curiosity, encouraging teamwork, and turning students into managers of their own learning. When students are taught to synthesize, assess, and evaluate their own achievement, education becomes more than something schools are doing to them; it becomes something they are doing for themselves and their futures.

- **Administrators set a tone of high expectations.**

One of the most challenging and difficult leadership roles is the management of expectations. The superintendent of education, for example, must not only set a tone of high expectations for students and staff, but also help parents and the community understand what they should expect and how they are expected to become involved as part of the team. This critical task is central to every administrator's role, from superintendent and central office administrator to principal.

- **No upper limits are placed on learning and achievement.**

When a student's interests and abilities exceed the existing curriculum, schools of the 21st century must help them break through what is often an artificially imposed ceiling. The student who is capable of going beyond what appear to be the limits may become frustrated if held back, and may actually lose interest.

That is why, as we enter the 21st century, many school systems have been allowing for continuous progress. For example, if a 6th grade student is capable of doing college-level math, many schools believe she should have the opportunity to do so and have the barriers removed that would have stopped her in the past. Some school systems want to extend gifted and talented education to all students, offering them an opportunity to excel far beyond traditional expectations. Some have worked out arrangements with local two- and four-year colleges to help these talented students move ahead. Again, the need for skilled and gifted teachers is paramount, teachers who are as comfortable learning from students as students are learning from them.

- **Assessment supports the learning process.**

Stephanie Pace Marshall, president of the Illinois Math and Science Academy, places this characteristic in perspective by commenting that "assessment is generated by the learning process." She adds, "The 21st century requires knowledge generation, not just information delivery. We need to create a culture of inquiry. We need to develop a new language if we hope to help students create new worlds."

A perennial criticism has been that the results of assessment find their way into a file but not necessarily into the improvement process. That is changing with a greater commitment to continuous improvement and to making assessment not an add-on, but a vital part of all education programs. In schools of the 21st century, each teacher will be responsible for clearly defining what is expected of the students in his class. Working together, students and teachers will know when a skill has been mastered or improvement is needed. Feedback will be instant.

Students, educators, parents, and the community will learn together, connected through their common interest in and need for constantly improving education.

ADDITIONAL CHARACTERISTICS: EFFECTIVE STANDARDS AND ASSESSMENT

Other characteristics in this category, identified by the Council of 21, include: teachers and administrators are assessed/self-assessed periodically in order to ensure continuous improvement; accountability includes the measurement of students' strengths and best performance; students demonstrate understanding and growth in learning; information delivery is based on multimedia, not just textbooks; assessments of student and staff performance are focused on continuous improvement of complex competencies; continuous improvement is institutionalized; teachers and principals are accountable for student achievement as measured in various disciplines; those closest to the classroom have a voice in policies and procedures; school boards and administrators understand and agree on goals for schools, teachers, and students; the school board determines accountability and the superintendent is responsible for ensuring leadership toward that accountability; school boards, with the participation of stakeholders, set the vision and policy while administrators are responsible for the operation of the system; the system is defined and organized around a framework of performance abilities required in career, civic, and family life; students emerge as productive workers as defined by employers and the economy; students use the community as a classroom, addressing and solving community issues and problems as part of the curriculum and are viewed as resources by the community; and the system provides analytic pathways for students to demonstrate understanding of essential knowledge and skills.

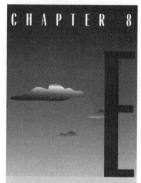

CHAPTER 8

Environmentally Responsive Infrastructure and Facilities

- A place of security and well-being—a safe haven for students and teachers.
- A safe place of joy and passion where children can explore and learn in a change-friendly culture that promotes innovation, healthy relationships, and success.
- A system with secure and adequate fiscal, material, and human resources.
- Information systems and structures that are continually updated to keep pace with rapid changes in technology.
- Constant, open access to information and resources that can guide learning.
- Flexibility that enables teachers to create different learning environments for students who learn in different ways.
- Schools as true community centers.
- A setting of academic excellence where exciting ideas fly from, to, and through bright teachers.
- Adequate technology available to all children in and out of school.
- Up-to-date, clean, and appropriately lighted physical plants with proper temperature control and air quality.
- A place where students want to be.

If I designed a school it would have lots of books, chalkboards and markers, a football field, a place for art, computers with Math Blasters and Encarta, and it would be a great big building.... We would have monkey bars everywhere on the inside and use them to go to our rooms. There would be a big curly slide to slide from the indoors to the outdoors, elevators and escalators, a glass roof all the way across the building, and lots of sunshine.

3rd Grader
Suncrest Elementary School
Frankfort, Kentucky 1997

Whenever we hear the word "school," we generally envision a building. It was that safe haven where we went to learn from dedicated teachers and got to know people who would become, in some cases, our lifelong friends. The school was and is the heart of the community.

As we move into the 21st century, we are faced with a double-dilemma. First, many of our nation's school facilities are desperately in need of repair. A recent study indicates that our country faces more than $112 billion in costs for deferred maintenance of school buildings. Second, the nature of the school facility, largely designed for an industrial age education, must change to help educators and communities deliver an education fit for students who will live their lives in a global knowledge/information age. School systems should be reshaping for the future, not making major investments in antiquity.

Many school systems are making strides in updating their school buildings and learning environments. Others, because of a lack of funds, foresight, or community will, still have the bulk of the work ahead of them.

Comments from the Council of 21 reflect the wide range of uses for and views about the importance of adequate school facilities for the 21st century.

"Place might not be as relevant in the future when we discuss the concept of school," says Michael Sullivan.

Adds Joseph Aguerrebere, "Our school facilities should contribute to the flexibility we need in managing our resources, such as time, space, materials, and so on."

"The school is the most efficient community site for the delivery of essential child welfare services of all kinds," says Stephen Heyneman. "These children are our future, and the school is where they can find people who care about them and their chances in life."

Above all, the school facility is a learning environment that either turns kids on or off to education. Growing new ideas in old structures presents a challenge; at the same time, a new building does not necessarily guarantee a new paradigm for education.

The following characteristics of environmentally responsive infrastructures and facilities for 21st century schools and school systems were identified by the Council of 21:

[Please note that several of these characteristics describe the ends themselves, such as "a place where children are safe to explore and learn," while others describe the means to an end, such as "adequate lighting and access to technology."]

- **A place of security and well-being—a safe haven for students and teachers.**

Effective schools research has proven over and over again that a safe and orderly environment is essential to learning. It is no wonder that safety and security rank at the

REINVIGORATING OUR SCHOOLS

The American Institute of Architects (AIA), in "Reinvigorating Our Schools," suggests six elements for discussion as school systems and their communities consider making improvements to school buildings. The guide suggests that stakeholders consider buildings' structural condition, environmental quality, size and capacity, safety and security, site location, and symbolic value and aesthetics.

Based on information from the U.S. Department of Education, "Reinvigorating Our Schools" predicts that by the first few years of the new century, K-12 enrollments will increase by 1.3 million.

top of Maslow's hierarchy of needs. In short, it's hard to learn, or even pay attention, when looking over your shoulder, fearing the worst.

As we approach the new millennium, incidents of violence are finding their way into school buildings and onto school grounds. As a result, some schools that once beckoned the community to freely visit have started requiring nametags for employees, installing metal detectors, and beefing up their security details. All of this, unfortunately, is deemed necessary to "protect" the school from the people it is meant to serve.

Students are more likely to prosper when their environment is conducive to learning. Architecture can be designed to support greater safety and security. Environmentally responsive heating, air conditioning, and ventilating systems, either in a new or renovated school, provide a more comfortable learning environment. Such well-designed systems send a powerful message to kids about he importance their community places on education.

"I believe the school facility should lend itself to the development of even better social skills among students," says Sam DeLay of the Tennessee Valley Authority. "Those social skills can contribute in a truly big way to overall security," he added.

- **A safe place of joy and passion where children can explore and learn in a change-friendly culture that promotes innovation, healthy relationships, and success.**

Schools should be exciting places. However, certain critics say the structure of many schools is more like a prison than a learning environment.

Anyone who enters a school should get a sense that the future is being shaped there, that people are working together toward lofty goals, and that the institution truly cares about children and the community.

Improving School Climate

Some refer to a "school's climate." What is climate? According to Jim Sweeney of Iowa State University, who wrote *Tips for Improving School Climate* (AASA 1988), it is "a term used to describe how people feel about their school. It is a combination of beliefs, values, and attitudes shared by students, teachers, parents, bus drivers, office personnel, custodians, cafeteria workers, and others who play an important role in the life of the school." Sweeney lists 10 characteristics associated with a winning school climate:

- A supportive, stimulating environment
- Student-centeredness
- Positive expectations
- Feedback
- Rewards
- A sense of family
- Closeness to parents and community
- Communication
- Achievement
- Trust

The culture of a school in the 21st century will send a message to the community and the world that, "No matter how good we are, you haven't seen anything yet."

- **A system with secure and adequate fiscal, material, and human resources.**

Building, maintaining, and upgrading school facilities, getting materials, and attracting staff all cost money. Communities, states, and nations that fail to provide an adequate level of financial and community support for reshaping their schools can expect their students and their communities to fall behind.

Because of a shortage of funds, many school systems have been forced to spend what they would normally allocate for maintenance and modification of their facilities on salaries and other essential bills. The situation has also lead to great disparities among schools across the nation in their abilities to gear up for technology and even to make their buildings more energy efficient.

In some communities, a local business may be willing to provide, at its expense, public school classrooms for children within its office building. The work-site school is just one example of the flexibility we might see as we consider making the most of fiscal, material, and human resources in the next century.

- **Information systems and structures that are continually updated to keep pace with rapid changes in technology.**

Donald Kussmaul expresses concern that, "the infrastructure of schools across the nation has been neglected for decades, most often in big cities." He adds, "We need to improve facilities for learning across the board, in big cities, in suburbs, and in rural and small school systems."

Stories abound about schools that have finally gotten computers into their classrooms, only to blow a fuse the minute they are plugged in. The upgrading of school facilities, including both electrical and communications wiring, is an essential step in preparing students for a global knowledge/information age. While school walls may look very much the same, they will actually become more transparent and porous as classrooms and individual students plug into the world. Schools must be designed to facilitate this change.

The design and construction of several new schools during the 1990s provides useful lessons in how to bring together students, teachers, parents, and community leaders to create wonderful places with technology infrastructures that engage and motivate learners to achieve high academic standards, and inspire even better teacher performance. (Several of these schools were selected to participate in this project. See the roster of "Gravity-Breaking Schools" in the Acknowledgments section of this book.)

Among the school systems that have recreated their school facilities for the 21st century is The Westside Community Schools in Omaha, Nebraska. Superintendent Kenneth Bird worked with staff and community to decide what students would need to learn and then designed technologically advanced school facilities that could support those rigorous and exciting plans.

- **Constant, open access to information and resources that can guide learning.**

Information is doubling globally every 18 months. According to Marvin Cetron, "80 percent of all engineers, scientists, chemists, physicists, and doctors who ever lived are alive today, and they're on the Internet."

Cetron adds, "We are beginning an interdisciplinary approach to solving our problems." Computer and information science is rapidly increasing in power, while prices are going down. Today, a $2000 computer is comparable to a $16 million computer a decade ago. Computer power has doubled 34 times since World War II, and probably will increase more than that by the time this publication makes it into print.

A challenge for schools and communities will be to make these technologies available to students and to use them in the education process. Access is a key factor if we hope to avoid a nation of technological haves and have-nots. Coupled with access is the need for a supportive physical infrastructure and professional development that make it possible for schools and school systems to put these new technologies to the most productive use. A further challenge is the constant need to upgrade these information and other technological resources.

- **Flexibility that enables teachers to create different learning environments for students who learn in different ways.**

School facilities should provide teachers a variety of possible spaces to enhance what is being taught and match students' learning styles. Facilities should provide venues where students can meet in small groups, conceive of ideas, explore theories, and do research, keeping in mind that some students learn best by hearing, others by seeing, and still others by doing.

As class sizes have declined in some school systems, overall enrollments have increased, making the demand for additional classroom space and quality teachers more intense. Each facility must provide appropriate space for individual learning, small-team activities, and large-group sessions, as well as places where students can readily connect to a variety of resources or to other learners who share their interests anywhere in the world.

- **Schools as true community centers.**

AASA Executive Director Paul Houston has made clear that school and school system leaders should be at the very crossroads of every community

GETTING PHYSICAL FACILITIES
READY FOR THE 21ST CENTURY
TEN TECHNICAL CONSIDERATIONS

1. **Deferred Maintenance.** Based on a 1995 U.S. General Accounting Office report, America's schools face $112 billion in deferred maintenance just to bring facilities up to date. Whether they are being renovated or newly constructed, schools will need to be brought up to standards that will allow them to serve students well in the 21st century.

2. **Technology Integration.** The schools' technology infrastructure should be totally integrated with community services. Ironically, many students who board the bus each morning leave at home their computer, direct broadcast satellite system, VCRs, DVDs, and electronic games and lessons.

3. **Electric Power.** Every room in a school must be wired for full technology capacity. A comprehensive plan should guide an electrical upgrade that might include multiple circuits to each classroom.

4. **Classroom Wiring.** Voice, video, data, and power lines must be run into the school and classroom in a safe, flexible, and efficient manner that is visually appealing and can be adapted to the changing needs of teaching and learning.

5. **Heating, Ventilating, Air Conditioning (HVAC), and Lighting.** In the GAO report, 36 percent of schools reported major problems in these areas. As more schools become community centers, offering activities from early morning until late in the evening, these issues will compound. Lighting becomes more critical as more computers and televisions are employed. Glare on various screens should be controlled through efficient lighting sources. Acoustic treatment of learning areas is an important design factor. New technologies make lighting and acoustical treatment more important than just comfort issues.

and that the schools should be the prime convener of the community as it addresses issues that affect children and their education.

In Houston's view, schools must increasingly become the heart of the communities they serve, through their web sites, newsletters, meeting facilities, and classes for people who hope to change careers or upgrade their skills. They will serve as centers for other community services. Lines will become blurred as school systems and community colleges focus on how they can best meet the needs of the whole community. Indeed, what we once called "schools" will become "community centers."

"Even when schools are in dangerous and run-down neighborhoods, they remain the safest haven for children and youth who may be sick, hungry, hurt,

6. **Indoor Air Quality (IAQ).** The Environmental Protection Agency has produced a kit of materials entitled "Tools for Schools" that provides excellent guidelines. It is possible to create a responsive environment that is both effective and avoids liabilities on the part of the school.

7. **Efficiency, Operations, and Maintenance.** More than 75 percent of American schools were built prior to 1970. Consequently, they were constructed before America "woke up" to the need for energy-efficient and environmentally responsive facilities. Schools and other facilities must be designed, upgraded, and operated efficiently in accordance with current HVAC standards.

8. **Investing Money Wisely.** Because of tight budgets, school systems are often faced with accepting the lowest bid. In purchasing equipment, this approach can mean low first costs but much higher operating costs over the long life of the equipment. A consideration should be made on the full "life-cycle" cost in all technology decisions, including the electric utility and telecommunications infrastructure. In areas of rapid change, school systems should consider the option to lease or buy.

9. **Food Service.** As community centers, more schools are offering food services all day—at breakfast, lunch, dinner, and sometimes in the evening. Innovations in food preparation can help school systems save money while continuing to ensure nutritious meals.

10. **Control Systems.** Schools need to be sure maintenance staffs have the skills and training they need to maintain and operate modern facilities. Those controls should be as simple as possible and should match the operational needs of the equipment, the changing schedule of the building, and the advice of architects and engineers.

abused, frightened, nervous or poor," says Heyneman. He goes on to say that the school is the most efficient environment for the delivery of many kinds of community services.

The best schools in the 21st century will be those most closely connected to their communities. That will mean keeping the school open from early morning until later in the evening for learning and recreational activities. It will mean that the school will become the site for a neighborhood or community-wide high tech network. A school may be connected to a joint-use city facility, such as a library, park, or recreation center.

To some extent, schools, by the very nature of their construction, are gathering points for the community. In smaller communities, for example, the school orchestra is the local symphony. Community educators and school public relations executives have long pointed out the need for connecting more closely with the community. After all, these valuable facilities are much too precious to be used just from September through June.

- **A setting of academic excellence where exciting ideas fly from, to, and through bright teachers.**

Marvin Cetron observes that teachers must be the catalysts in setting a culture of academic excellence. They must create within their own sphere of influence an understanding of greatness and a desire within their students to excel. An individual teacher often sees in a student the promise that others overlook. Over the years many of our highest achievers have thanked that inspired teacher who was able to kindle sparks of greatness.

"The setting or culture should support and encourage academic excellence," says Sophie Sa.

- **Adequate technology available to all children in and out of school.**

Our classrooms should be at least as well equipped as our students' living rooms. Unfortunately, too many schools lack adequate infrastructure to support technology.

Infrastructures must be planned to provide an ability to communicate to the desktop, to the home, and around the world. Schools must think about the purchase or leasing of technology infrastructures as operational investments in learning rather than as capital costs. Those investments go beyond hardware, software, and training to adequate electrical power and computer jacks. And we must add to that the need to be prepared for wireless and the upcoming conversion to digital television with its 9 x 16 ratio.

- **Up-to-date, clean, and appropriately lighted physical plants with proper temperature control and air quality.**

School leaders should work constantly with architects and engineers to ensure that their physical plants, their learning environments for students, are up-to-date, clean, and appropriately lighted, with well-controlled temperature and air quality.

As a general rule, according to the Thomas Jefferson Center for Educational Design, Curry School of Education, at the University of Virginia, schools should:

  — Be exemplary of technology, sustainability, and accountability;
  — Direct students to activities;
  — Evoke a spirit of place;
  — Teach; and
  — Affect positive change in education.

- **A place where students want to be.**

Children are attracted to schools that are learner-centered and equipped so that they can explore and achieve at high levels. We have challenged some children in sports, music, drama, and science fairs to be actively engaged at school. We must now extend this challenge to learning for all children.

"We should create schools that stimulate students to say 'yes' when asked, 'Do you want to come back tomorrow?'" says Les Omotani.

Adds Kimberly Cetron, "The physical environment should also be a motivational environment."

* * *

Our children are our future. Our investment in them and in their school facilities is an investment that will pay huge dividends as we move into the 21st century.

ADDITIONAL CHARACTERISTICS: ENVIRONMENTALLY RESPONSIVE INFRASTRUCTURE AND FACILITIES

The Council of 21 suggested nearly 20 additional characteristics for environmentally responsive infrastructure and facilities, many of which have been covered in other items in this chapter. These characteristics state that the school's infrastructure provides: technology that is equally available to all children in and out of school; a place of respect; school days and a school year that are generally longer than before the year 2000; mechanisms for identifying, protecting, and supporting children who are neglected or abused; a setting where children are uplifted in terms of ideas, challenges, and relationships; a drug-free environment; an emphasis on flexible use of time; alternatives times and places for learning; a system that operates organically with all parts relating to and enriching other parts synergistically; visionaries, not just tenured staff, who design new schools; laptop computers supplied to all students; a year-round school model; improvements in infrastructure with support from businesses, especially in the area of computer availability; a minimum of 190 days of instruction per year; and partnership spaces.

CHAPTER 9

School – Community Linkages

- Parents are engaged in the learning process – for their children's education as well as their own.
- Schools are "around-the-clock" hubs for lifelong learning that enhance education and achievement for everyone in the community.
- Investing in education is supported by all corporate and community leaders.
- Teachers and parents work together to increase student performance.
- Schools are linked to healthcare, housing, social service, and other community agencies.
- Parents clearly understand their responsibilities.
- Learning experiences occur within a framework of real-life issues and challenges.
- Students are engaged in community service, service learning, and work experience.
- Educators bring expertise and resources from the community into the schools.
- Schools are connected electronically with the world-at-large and serve as community learning centers.

Children and youth require the following resources: an ongoing relationship with a caring adult, safe places and structured activities during non-school hours, a healthy start, a marketable skill through effective education, and an opportunity to give back through community service.

The five basic resources to be delivered by schools and communities to children and youth through America's Promise—The Alliance for Youth

How effectively schools educate students has a profound impact on a community's future. At the same time, how well a community supports its schools will determine, in large measure, how effective they can be. In short, schools and school systems are inextricably linked to the communities they serve, and vice versa.

School–community links are brought to life in many ways. Community education programs help schools serve a broader constituency, often providing learning opportunities for children and adults, and turning the school into a center for community services. Community or public relations programs work to ensure that the system is listening to the people it serves and providing information that builds understanding and responds to problems. School–business–community partnerships help schools link what they teach to real life and often enable school to gain additional resources.

The following characteristics of school-community linkages for schools and school systems of the 21st century were identified by the Council of 21:

- **Parents are engaged in the learning process — for their children's education as well as their own.**

Harold Howe applauds engaging parents in the learning process, not only for the sake of their children, but for their own education as well. While parents' time may be limited because of employment and other commitments, they can still provide a wellspring of information for the school and help their children understand how their education connects to real life. At the same time, parents and others in the community can pursue anything from a course in parenting skills to preparation for a new career, all offered at this community hub we call school.

- **Schools are "around-the-clock" hubs for lifelong learning that enhance education and achievement for everyone in the community.**

Schools represent a substantial community investment. For decades, people have wondered how such valuable resources could be allowed to hum with activity all day and go dark at night. Many have found the answer in the "lighted school," a term used to signify schools used day and night as learning and recreation centers. In the 21st century, schools must also become digital hubs, which will be open electronically 24 hours a day, 7 days a week, 365 days a year. One product of this approach will be intergenerational understanding and support.

Some people have even suggested that, as baby boomers get older, schools should consider offering geriatric daycare and providing a community gathering point for older citizens. For example, the Lake Worth School District in Houston, Texas, takes pride in being open from 6 a.m. until 10 p.m., offering childcare and computer programs for adults. It also offers a cooperative program with the University of Texas that provides leadership certification for teachers with at least five years of service in the school system.

"When people are regularly in their schools, safety, cleanliness, and up-to-date equipment become issues for the entire community," says Nancy Stover.

Monica Bradsher adds, "A byproduct of this approach will be broader community support and fuller use of school facilities connected to what people need, such as lifelong learning and preparation for multiple career changes."

- **Investing in education is supported by all corporate and community leaders.**

Education is not an expense. It is an investment. Corporate and community leaders need to understand and support this basic concept.

In the 21st century, superintendents must help their communities see the school system as the very crossroads of the community. They will reach out to business and community leaders, often meeting them on their turf, but also making sure those leaders and citizens at-large have real-life experience in the schools.

Business and community leaders will also be connected to valuable information about the education system through newsletters and online services. Their views will be sought individually and through advisory groups on issues that have communitywide implications.

When community and business leaders have an opportunity to tell educators directly about their need for global knowledge/ information age workers and sound citizens, educators have an equal opportunity to tell them about the support they will need to make that possible.

Sandra Welch, former senior vice president of education for PBS, emphasizes the need for corporate leaders to work with educators to bring the work of the Council of 21 to life in school systems across the nation.

- **Teachers and parents work together to increase student performance.**

Parents want their students to perform at high levels. While their time is often limited, the collective expertise of parents can help teachers enrich what happens in the classroom and connect it to real life. School generally takes on added meaning for students who know their parents value education enough to get involved.

"Schools will be much more successful in preparing students for the 21st century if parents and other caregivers are part of the process," according the Arnold Fege, president of Public Advocacy for Kids and a longtime staff member of the National PTA.

- **Schools are linked to healthcare, housing, social service, and other community agencies.**

As businesses and some other institutions have moved toward continuous improvement, they have decided that helpfulness and friendliness to clients is essential. Now, people expect it from public institutions as well.

Parents and other citizens demand, and rightfully so, more user-friendly public institutions. Their lives are busy and their time is valuable. That's why some school systems are inviting community agencies that provide health, housing, social, family, and other community services to place their offices in local schools, closer to their clients.

This approach provides "one-stop shopping" for services communities need, says Klaus Driessen, former superintendent of Lake Worth Independent School District in Houston, Texas.

Donald Fiedler, superintendent of Academy School District #20 in Colorado Springs, Colorado, cautions that "the services offered by these agencies need to be assessed not by the schools, but by another appropriate community agency."

In the new century, many of these services will be linked through a communitywide web site, often anchored at the local school.

- **Parents clearly understand their responsibilities.**

It's one thing to say schools need parental support. It's another to meet with parents and agree on what that support might include. Obviously, parents should take responsibility for nurturing their children; providing adequate food, clothing, and shelter; and promoting their physical and mental health. In the 21st century, schools and parents must also discuss and agree on their individual and shared responsibilities for each child's education. "All parties need to understand their responsibilities if we are to become fully successful in educating children," says John O'Rourke.

- **Learning experiences occur within a framework of real-life issues and challenges.**

The Council of 21 asserts that students need to see the connection between what they are studying in school and real-life problems and issues. 21st century schools will see an increase in project-based learning that reaches out to the workplace and the civic community. Most educators do not have direct experience in the private sector and some, because of limited time, may not be

HOW PARENTS CAN HELP THEIR KIDS...SUPPORT THEIR LEARNING

- Become a member of your school's parent-teacher organization.

- Help with a project, ranging from lending a hand in the library to helping set up a computer.

- Visit a class to talk about your career.

- Invite a class to visit your workplace.

- Attend school-sponsored events, such as performances and athletic events.

- Serve on committees and/or run for the school board.

- Talk to your child about the importance of education.

Adapted from *Parenting Skills...Bringing Out the Best in Your Child*, AASA 1989; revised 1999.

able to participate in appointed or elected community boards and committees. For them and for their students, these projects can provide valuable links to the community.

- **Students are engaged in community service, service learning, and work experience.**

Young people, especially teenagers, have the ability to function at high levels in their communities. There are many examples of children performing in community theaters, participating in science fairs, and performing at a high level in activities ranging from concert violinist to cancer researcher. The *USA Today* "All USA Academic Team," the Discover Card Tribute Awards, Prudential's "Spirit of Community" Awards, and the annual Caring Institute Awards provide magnificent examples of the positive effect students can have on their communities.

As we enter the new century, schools must expand these connections through appropriate and carefully directed community service, service learning, and work experience programs. From these experiences, students will gain first-hand knowledge of how their communities and businesses work. All students, prior to engaging in these activities, should be prepared to make a contribution, exhibit good work habits, observe functions ranging from budgets to ethics, and to act responsibly.

- **Educators bring expertise and resources from the community into the schools.**

Collaboration is replacing competition as we head into the 21st century. What we can't do adequately on our own, we can often accomplish through working together, sharing information, ideas, and experience. A community, by its very nature, offers a treasure trove of opportunities for schools not only to stay in touch, but to get things done. Larry Decker, a respected expert in community education, observes in the AASA publication *Getting Parents Involved in Their Children's Education* (1994) that some educators like to keep parents and the community "at arms length." That tendency must be overcome.

Growing numbers of businesses and other institutions want to demonstrate their social responsibility, and the schools provide an ideal venue. Joint school/community efforts are generally more effective when they are supported by a partnership agreement spelling out who is expected to do what. They are sustained by frequent communication, teamwork, and recognition.

- **Schools are connected electronically with the world-at-large and serve as community learning centers.**

In the 21st century, rarely will we find a school without a web page or e-mail services. Many will not only have access to interactive cable, but will be among the primary planners in making these new systems work for the schools and the community. Growing numbers of schools will be expected to perform as community learning centers connected electronically to the world-at-large.

During the last decade of the 20th century, cable operators, online services, and other electronic industry groups have been working, in many cases voluntarily, to "wire" schools. Through the Universal Services Act, funding was made available to many schools that needed a financial boost to get that job done.

On the technical and business sides, school systems must have long-term plans for the installation and effective use of technology and the telecommunications infrastructures. Those plans will include objectives for the technology, the anticipated maintenance and operational costs, and the expected life cycle of the equipment. Fulfilling these long-term plans will ensure that 21st century schools are community learning centers that serve as windows to the world.

ADDITIONAL CHARACTERISTICS: SCHOOL-COMMUNITY LINKAGES

In addition to the items included in this chapter, members of the Council of 21 identified these additional characteristics of 21st century schools providing school-community linkages: schools serve as community learning centers with adults using computer facilities for continuing education and recreation on nights and weekends; innovative school-business partnerships expand resources and enhance the capability of the teaching staff; productive learning takes place beyond the K-12 setting and outside regular school hours; economic disparity between and among communities is addressed by way of educational parity; the community is "built into schools" with working groups of students focusing on academic, cultural, and ethical conduct; school is a place in an international/global community where students learn from resources available anywhere in the world; learning experiences extend beyond the boundaries of the school's attendance area; there are strong, ongoing links with the community, not limited to a geographic area; education is intergenerational; school is any place where individuals join together to learn; and schools launch other learning sites in the community.

nformation/Knowledge Age Teaching

- There is extensive preparation, professional development, and support for teachers, from preservice through lifelong education.

- Teachers are expected to pursue continuous learning and to expand their personal knowledge.

- The faculty is well prepared in both content and learning theory.

- Teachers serve as facilitators and moderators, not just providers of information and subject matter specialists.

- Teachers are prepared to teach students from diverse cultures and backgrounds.

- Incompetent teachers are removed in a timely fashion.

- Teachers are prepared in multiple uses of technology.

- Teachers are the best and brightest people society has to offer.

- Teachers conduct and respect themselves as true professionals.

- Teachers are knowledgeable about the subject areas they teach.

"I have touched the future...I teach."

That poignant and powerful declaration by Christa McAuliffe, the teacher who lost her life in the Challenger disaster, carries a powerful message. The future of the United States of America has always been in the hands of those who teach.

As we move into the 21st century, U.S. teachers have been shifting from the "Sages on the Stage" to "Guides on the Side," as they define a new genre of educational professionals who are academic coaches. In the global knowledge/information age, the expectation will continue to grow that all students will perform at a high level of mastery. Teachers will be challenged not only to provide information, but to help students turn that information into usable knowledge, and ultimately into wisdom. Already as we move into the new century, growing numbers of teachers are seeking national certification through the National Board for Professional Teaching Standards.

In the 19th century, Horace Mann fought for the rights of all children to benefit from education. His work brought a landmark shift in educational philosophy and practice. In the 21st century, armed with new knowledge about learning styles, a vast arsenal of electronic tools, and growing support for even better education, teachers may breathe even more life into Mann's dream.

How important is teaching to the American people? In a 1998 poll conducted by Louis Harris for

Recruiting New Teachers, Inc., "roughly 9 out of 10 Americans said the way to lift student achievement is to ensure a qualified teacher in every classroom."

MORE KIDS ... MORE COMPETITION FOR TEACHERS

The U. S. Department of Education estimates that the United States will need 2,000,000 new K-12 teachers by the year 2006. The demand for lifelong learning may swell that need even further. The concept of cradle-to-grave education opportunities for all extends teaching and learning to the workplace, civic and professional organizations, television, and the Internet. The rise in telecourses, netcourses, and non-traditional courses is making it possible for formal learning to take place anywhere, anytime, and at any pace. The pathway to learning no longer goes only to the schoolhouse door. This alone could increase the competition schools and school systems face in attracting the brightest and best into the classroom.

The following characteristics of 21st schools and school systems pursuing information/knowledge age teaching were identified by the Council of 21:

- **There is extensive preparation, professional development, and support for teachers, from preservice through lifelong education.**

All educators, including teachers, must be better prepared. Colleges and universities need to provide prospective teachers not only with theory but also with front-line experiences that prepare them for a broad range of students in various types of communities. Too many first-year teachers call it quits because they aren't ready for the rigors of the classroom.

Getting ready is one thing. Keeping up is another. Teachers need ongoing professional development. Some of that development will happen through workshops, advisory committees, and professional organizations. Interactive professional development programs will also be offered online and through distance learning. And professional development schools will provide an opportunity for those just out of college to work with master teachers.

Twenty-first century teachers will be a mix of scholar, content expert, front-line information specialist, team leader, and motivator. The very best will inspire their students to want to learn, creating in each of them a thirst for knowledge. "If we hope to have great schools, then global knowledge/information age preparation and professional development will be essential," says Marilyn Mathis.

- **Teachers are expected to pursue continuous learning and to expand their personal knowledge.**

"Everyone else in the workforce is pursuing continuous learning and growth, and their companies pay for it. Who pays for the teachers?" asks Nancy Stover.

"We talk about lifelong learning for everyone in society. We need to be sure that we offer lifelong learning for our teachers," adds Marvin Cetron.

"Professional development should be coupled with constant growth in personal knowledge, which enriches education for students," says Katie Mulholland.

- **The faculty is well prepared in both content and learning theory.**

Schools of education must create an intellectually rich environment in which they prepare teachers for the rigors of teaching and learning in the 21st century. In preparing teachers and administrators, college and university faculty should apply the types of real-world experiences and tools they expect those educators to use when they move into the K-12 environment.

SKILLS AND KNOWLEDGE OF OUTSTANDING TEACHERS FROM NASA'S CLASSROOM OF THE FUTURE

In a position paper for the NASA Classroom of the Future, Frank B. Withrow listed skills and knowledge that help make teachers outstanding. These include:

- A major interest in the development of high academic achievement of all students and a deep commitment to their education.
- An understanding of basic symbol systems, phonetics, linguistics, mathematics, and technology.
- A command of computer and information sciences.
- A dynamic understanding of content areas ranging from history to physics.
- Access at home and in libraries and classrooms to the Internet and other telecommunications resources.
- An expressive and receptive ability to use multimedia resources.
- An ability to adapt in-depth software programs to problem-based learning.
- An ability to allow students to interact with simulations and solve problems.
- An ability to maintain and keep pace with developments in their content areas.
- An ability to integrate academic achievement into the healthy social and emotional development of young people.
- An ability to team teach with on-site and distance learning teachers.
- An ability to quickly identify students who are performing inadequately and provide the needed technical and human support required to motivate them to learn.
- An ability to assimilate skills and knowledge into a global perspective.

"Some teachers know the material, but they don't know how to get it across," says Callie Langohr.

Kimberly Cetron emphasizes that a command of both content and learning theory is important.

- **Teachers serve as facilitators and moderators, not just providers of information and subject matter specialists.**

"Orchestrators of learning." That's how some people describe the 21st century teacher. When these teachers walk into the classroom, they can assume that many of their students have been surfing the web, and that they are loaded with information and curious about what it means. These teachers can also assume that some students will lack access to or interest in the world of information that is virtually at their fingertips. And because the community will expect all students to achieve, teachers will be charged with monitoring results and providing constant guidance.

While information will continue to be a teacher's stock-in-trade, it won't be enough. Teachers will cajole their students to think about how certain information might be put to use, which is an important step in helping them develop knowledge. Teachers will also stimulate students to think about what information means, which is a prime step in helping students develop wisdom.

Like any successful leaders, teachers will serve as moderators and facilitators, helping their charges connect with additional information and people, including their fellow students. And teachers will guide students toward projects that help them apply their knowledge in real-life situations. At the same time, they will help students understand what is expected, and they'll work hard to help them become self-learners.

- **Teachers are prepared to teach students from diverse cultures and backgrounds.**

Nothing is quite so American as diversity. It enriches our nation. At the same time, it challenges teachers to become adept at motivating and educating children who come from every part of the globe and who are diverse in every imaginable way.

In school districts where students from a single group make up nearly 100 percent of the ethnic profile, teachers and administrators may feel little need to offer programs and activities that help students understand and appreciate people of other cultures and backgrounds. However, those same students, when they leave school, will enter a world of diversity, and they will realize that they have been deprived.

Therefore, through their preparation at colleges and universities, through professional development programs, and through community activities, teachers and all other school personnel need to understand how diversity can enrich a school or community and how they can help students understand and value diversity.

- **Incompetent teachers are removed in a timely fashion.**

We sometimes think that those most concerned about problem teachers are students, parents, and administrators. In fact, those most concerned are often other highly professional teachers. This issue was ranked high in impact by the Council of 21, which also expresses a high level of doubt that the problem will be solved in the near term. While enrollments are growing, many teachers are leaving the classroom for better paying jobs in business and industry. As a result, many school systems are forced to retain teachers who don't measure up.

In the 21st century, as expectations continue to skyrocket, the penalty for ineffective teaching will become so great that school systems and teacher organizations will have to work together more closely to ensure that only those who are qualified and competent continue to teach. One member of the Council of 21 calls tenure "the greatest impediment to improvement." Another reminds us that tenure is designed only "to protect teachers from arbitrary dismissal and other such abuses."

- **Teachers are prepared in multiple uses of technology.**

New technologies bring to the classroom an impressive array of possibilities unimagined just a few years ago. They provide a virtual window on the world. However, these technologies are not a panacea. Their effectiveness depends, to a great extent, on teachers who know what technology to use and when and how to use it. Therefore, at every level of preparation and professional development, teachers and administrators must be helped to understand the benefits of various technologies and how to actually use them.

Gary Rowe, a longtime leader in technology, cautions school systems not to throw the baby out with the bath water. "There are things that have worked and will continue to work because of the knowledge and instructional skills of teachers. Mastering technology solely for the sake of technology isn't enough. What we need is for teachers to

SPECIALTY HIGH SCHOOLS

Specialty high schools are becoming an important part of the education scene as we move toward a new century. A number of excellent schools for the performing arts have developed around the nation as well as special science, mathematics, and technology programs, including North Carolina's Governor Hunt School; the Illinois Mathematics and Science Academy; Louisiana's Science, Mathematics, and Performing Arts School; the Duke Ellington School for Performing Arts in Washington, D.C.; and Virginia's Thomas Jefferson High School for Science and Technology.

understand the power and limitations of technologies and to use them only when appropriate."

- **Teachers are the best and brightest people society has to offer.**

One way to ensure that the best and brightest are attracted to teaching and stay with it, according to Kimberly Cetron, "is to raise teaching to a higher level of professionalism rather than treating it as child care." She predicts that "By virtue of increased professionalism, salary and public respect will follow."

Phyllis Tate, principal of Einstein Elementary School in Chicago, expresses concern that educators' salaries need to become competitive with business and industry. "Since education is supported by taxes, not private funds, this issue regrettably may be unresolved as we move into the 22nd century," she says.

As Tate reminds us, school systems face stiff competition as they attempt to recruit the best and brightest into education careers. Some are doing extensive recruiting. Others are offering incentives, often provided by the community. Some are trying to convince people from outside education who want to add significance to their lives to consider preparing themselves for a teaching career. Some are trying to make teaching more attractive by offering wellness programs and other internal incentives. Ultimately, salaries and working conditions must be improved as competition for qualified persons to educate our children comes from multiple sources, not just other school systems.

High Tech Teacher Prep...A Future View

Teacher preparation programs may want to use this description as a starting point as they discuss how to get from where they are to where they need to be.

From the day they enter a preparation program, prospective teachers should have their own personal laptop computers. Learning environments in colleges and universities for teacher preparation should have large screen displays and LANs, allowing students to plug into the classroom system. Student teachers must have virtual simulated classrooms allowing them to interact with different teaching strategies and conditions. All dormitory rooms for student teachers should have Internet connectivity. Teacher preparation colleges and universities must provide technical support staff to allow prospective teachers to prepare materials in digital formats, including full-motion picture, graphic, and sound production. Finally, teachers in preparation must have access to digital libraries with abundant teaching and learning resources.

- **Teachers conduct and respect themselves as true professionals.**

Who are the outstanding teachers? Some say they are people who respect themselves and conduct themselves as true professionals. They are the people who not only know the subject matter, but who also have the ability to inspire the students they teach. True professionals are confident in their skills and knowledge. They believe in themselves and their contributions to children and society, yet they are constantly committed to improving, no matter how good they are.

Many teachers feel they are not treated professionally because they do not have direct access to telephones and computers and have no office space to call their own. "Teaching should be promoted as a profession, within the full meaning of the word professional," says Harold Howe.

- **Teachers are knowledgeable about the subject areas they teach.**

Too often, teachers are assigned to cover classes outside their fields of expertise. Generally, these assignments are made because of a shortage of people who are fully qualified

> *It is natural for teachers to teach as they have been taught.*

in given areas. As we move into the 21st century, schools and school systems must match educators' capabilities and qualifications with the job at hand. Professional development must be offered to constantly upgrade the knowledge and abilities of teachers and to help them and, ultimately, their students be successful.

ADDITIONAL CHARACTERISTICS: INFORMATION/KNOWLEDGE AGE TEACHING

The Council of 21 also identified and considered the following characteristics directly related to information/knowledge age teaching: teaching is promoted as a profession; the rigor of teacher preparation and licensure command the respect of the public and talented, diverse Americans; teachers undergo apprenticeship programs that ensure that they are well-trained and knowledgeable; a school principal is primarily an instructional leader; highly motivated and competent mentors are available to teachers and students; teachers are paid on merit and not on experience; teachers must apply for meaningful recertification at various points in their careers and are rewarded for continuous certification; teachers are challenged not just to provide information but also to help students develop knowledge and wisdom; teachers are held in high esteem by society; students and teachers learn to construct knowledge in response to problems that have real-world applications and solutions; teachers are treated as professionals whose opinions are sought; and schools tap the knowledge and experience of retirees.

CHAPTER 11

Responsive Governance, Targeted Funding, and Research-Based Improvement

School leaders create strong schools. Research and common sense suggest that administrators can do a great deal to advance school reform. I believe they must and will lead the second wave of reform.

Bill Clinton
Governor of Arkansas 1991

Section 1: Responsive Governance

Section 1: Responsive Governance

- The entire educational system, from the classroom to the federal government, is focused on the needs of learners, parents, and society.
- Governance is stable, with school boards focusing on the common goal of providing quality learning.
- Leadership is collaborative.
- Teachers and principals have flexibility and control over what they need to effectively run their classrooms and schools.
- The system's central office focuses on facilitation and capacity-building rather than command and control.
- Well-managed, empowered staff is consulted in decision making.
- Administrators are skillful leaders who win the respect of other professionals.
- Decision making is collaborative and exhibits a balance of power.
- Education is increasingly deregulated, allowing excellent teaching to replace mediocrity.
- The accomplishments of students and staff are celebrated.

School governance in the United States develops and is guided by a combination of local, state, and federal laws, regulations, court rulings, and policies. Too often, local, state, and federal authorities become adversaries at the very time when creative partnerships are needed among these levels of government, in concert with professional educators.

The United States has a national interest in education, state responsibility for education, and local leadership of education. It is a decentralized system, and rather unique among the education systems of the world.

Schools for yesterday were designed and operated for the community with very defined core programs of reading, writing, and arithmetic. For most students, this was a rudimentary education. It gave them the foundation to learn many things.

Schools for today are designed for a more complex and wider range of societal goals and objectives as well as expanded basic core academic content. Many more advanced placement content programs are now available to many students.

Schools for the 21st century must emphasize the learner, and be flexible enough to enable all students to achieve high academic mastery.

The following characteristics of a responsive school governance system for the 21st century were identified by the Council of 21:

- **The entire educational system, from the classroom to the federal government, is focused on the needs of learners, parents, and society.**

The system of governance must encourage and support, not mandate and neglect. When education becomes a popular public issue, candidates for public office stake their campaigns on ways they will fix the system. What is needed is not a fix for a system of education that prepares students for an industrial age, but creation of a system capable of preparing students for a global knowledge/information age.

The governance system must help educators and communities solve their problems, not just create new ones. According to one member of the Council of 21, unless the governance system helps schools and educators address their real needs, then it might end up, in one way or another, opposing nearly every item on the 21st century agenda.

Leadership is required at all levels of governance to support schools as they create a renewed system of education. That leadership should be thoughtful and avoid quick fixes and political jargon. Working in concert with professional educators, it should focus on the needs of learners, parents, and society and help move the system of education to even greater heights.

- **Governance is stable, with school boards focusing on the common goal of providing quality learning.**

The Council of 21 agrees that school boards should not dwell on special interests. Instead, they should focus on policies that support the larger interests of education for all students in the community. There should be continuity in the relationship between the board and superintendent. Positive, trusting, supportive relationships are needed to make it possible for schools and school systems to prepare students for the 21st century.

While noting that school boards are not likely to be replaced, Phillip Schlechty, president of the Center for Leadership in School Reform in Louisville, Ky., says boards should make an effort to "eliminate politics in favor of a continuity of purpose."

- **Leadership is collaborative.**

As the entire workforce, including teachers, becomes better educated, management will be expected to give all staff an opportunity to express their ideas, share their experiences, and have a voice in decision making. The world is moving from competition to collaboration, and schools must join the move. "Interdependence, counting on each other, might describe the relationship," says Harold Brewer.

- **Teachers and principals have flexibility and control over what they need to effectively run their classrooms and schools.**

Members of the Council of 21, while supporting the concept of providing greater flexibility and control to schools and classrooms, cautions that standards must be met and everyone must be accountable for results. While states may exercise more control in setting standards and assessments, teachers will control how those standards are best met. Flexibility offers breathing room and the opportunity for greater creativity, but it can't leave the process unmonitored, according to Callie Langohr. On the other hand, teachers and principals with greater flexibility and control "must also have the support they need to be successful," adds Nancy Stover.

- **The system's central office focuses on facilitation and capacity-building rather than command and control.**

"I believe that site-based decision making can create an environment that helps ensure that students' educational needs will be met," says Phillip Schoo, superintendent of the Lincoln Public Schools in Nebraska. Indeed, school system central office leaders are moving away from command and control and toward facilitation, capacity building, and involvement.

"In business and industry and in other organizations such as government, command and control governance is on its way out," says Gary Rowe.

- **Well-managed, empowered staff is consulted in decision making.**

This characteristic, identified by the Council of 21, is essential in any well-managed organization, whether it is a school system, a business, a nonprofit group, or a unit of government.

- **Administrators are skillful leaders who win the respect of other professionals.**

Administrators of 21st century schools must be leaders in the very best sense. They will take the lead in setting a vision and in offering direction, guidance, recognition, credit, and support to everyone in the system, including the community. These thoughtful statespersons will be intellectual leaders who help others solve their own problems. "A leader is often the person who, when confronted with a problem, issue, or opportunity, connects the people who can deal with it," says Paul Houston.

- **Decision making is collaborative and exhibits a balance of power.**

In many ways, schools are a reflection of the communities they serve. When decision making is collaborative and inclusive, a school system can maintain policies and procedures that help it keep up with a fast-changing world of new ideas, diverse cultures, and new people.

- **Education is increasingly deregulated, allowing excellent teaching to replace mediocrity.**

The governance of schools, while primarily centered in the local community, must involve a positive working partnership that enables rather than inhibits excellence at every level of education. Local, state, and federal government all play a part. For example, certain mandates might inappropriately skew the curriculum; old policies and procedures might inhibit progress.

Stephen Heyneman calls on governance to lessen the confusion by having decisions made collaboratively or at the most appropriate level. For example, he suggests that decisions on performance standards be largely made at the central level, while decisions on pedagogy and syllabi be made at the local school level. However, the Council agrees that simply deregulating will not turn a mediocre teacher or school into a great one. Other actions must accompany this one.

- **The accomplishments of students and staff are celebrated.**

Recognition of accomplishment is like fuel to most human beings. Everyone needs some level of feedback. The late H. Vaughn Phelps, who served as superintendent of The Westside Community Schools in Omaha, Neb., and as president of AASA, was fond of saying of staff, "I want each one to be able to paint a picket fence, and I want the whole world to know who painted it."

ADDITIONAL CHARACTERISTICS: RESPONSIVE GOVERNANCE

Other characteristics of a responsive governance system for 21st century schools and school systems identified by the Council of 21 include: school boards and superintendents appreciate each other's respective roles and responsibilities; union calls for collaboration at the national level are reflected at the local level; there is an ability to change programs, content, and all other elements on a daily basis; and the aspirations of each group of interested communities are fulfilled, while maintaining a shared sense of loyalty and mutual obligations for social compromise. Some items called for change in the way school boards govern as a means of paving the way for preparing schools and school systems for the 21st century.

PREPARING SCHOOLS AND SCHOOL SYSTEMS FOR THE 21ST CENTURY

Section 2: Targeted Funding

Nothing passes from a lower level of government, for example, the local to the state or the state to the federal, unless that lower level of government has abdicated its responsibility.

Otto Kerner
Governor of Illinois 1964

Section 2: Targeted Funding

- Adequate and equitably distributed funding is available to provide high-quality education for all children.
- Curriculum is funded based on a clear set of specific learning goals that lead to literacy in reading, writing, mathematics, science, and other subjects.
- An appropriate pupil-teacher ratio enhances learning for all students.
- Salaries of teachers, principals, and superintendents are commensurate with their great societal worth.
- Adequate resources are focused on the weakest learners.
- Additional incentives encourage the best teachers to work with the most disadvantaged children.
- An investment in basic and applied research supports educational reform.
- Incentives are provided to attract members of minority groups into the teaching profession as educators and role models.
- Teachers are paid based on merit.
- Technology replaces textbooks as the primary instructional medium.

Elementary and secondary education in America is a multi-billion dollar industry. As we move into the 21st century, demands on schools and schools systems will continue to grow; expectations will continue to rise; and financial support will continue to be needed.

In the late 1990s, nearly 14,000 school systems, with approximately 107,000 schools and nearly 3 million educators, are serving more than 50 million students.

In 1970-71, on average, 8.4 percent of funds for elementary and secondary education came from the federal government, 39.1 percent from state government, and 52.5 percent from local government. By 1994-95, 6.8 percent of funding came from federal sources, 46.8 percent from the state, and 46.4 percent from the local level. In short, funding from the state level has increased on a percentage basis, while funding from federal and local levels has declined. Much of that change came as an effort to equalize educational opportunity among communities. According to the General Accounting Office (GAO), the United States perennially ranks low among countries in its percentage of gross national product (GNP) devoted to education. In 1993-1994 the United States invested only the equivalent of 4.5 percent of its GNP in elementary and secondary schools.

As schools prepare students for a global knowledge/information age, they are focusing on the needs of all students, in the best American tradition. Moving forward and maintaining our democratic

77

society will require an educated citizenry. It always has, and it always will.

Each community, each state, and the nation must provide financial support to sustain the forward momentum of schools as they prepare students for a new century.

The following characteristics of 21st century school systems focused on the need for targeted funding were identified by the Council of 21:

- **Adequate and equitably distributed funding is available to provide high-quality education for all children.**

"Adequate funding may not be equitably distributed," cautions Arnold Fege. He adds, "Financial support should be provided to meet the needs of the individual child. Some children, because of the nature of education and their developmental needs, may require more resources than others." In the new century, a clear and effective sharing of national, state, and local resources must become a reality for all schools and school systems.

"Somehow, we're going to have to get past having people in the corporate and government communities telling us to do more with less," asserts Kenneth Bird, superintendent of The Westside Community Schools in Omaha, Nebraska. "While the tension might be healthy, we all need to be on the same team as we try to shape education to prepare our kids for the 21st century."

- **Curriculum is funded based on a clear set of specific learning goals that lead to literacy in reading, writing, mathematics, science, and other subjects.**

Research has given us information about how various children learn best. The challenge is to obtain the support needed to make our new understandings common practice. In order to attract needed funding, schools and school systems must identify their aims and clearly communicate to their communities why additional support is needed.

- **An appropriate pupil-teacher ratio enhances learning for all students.**

Class size and pupil-teacher ratios have been a topic of debate for decades. Perhaps the argument is unsettled because there is no one best answer that fits every community and the needs of all students. In the 21st century, the question might shift to how many professionals with particular knowledge and skills are needed to help students learn in a variety of situations, from large-group to small-group to individual settings, based on what is being taught and individual students' learning styles and needs. Meanwhile, the work of teachers will continue to be enhanced by community and technological resources and supported by content and technical experts.

- **Salaries of teachers, principals, and superintendents are commensurate with their great societal worth.**

The American people have long demonstrated that they are willing to pay for what they value in society. Linda Darling-Hammond of Stanford University has headed a long-term study of teachers. Not surprisingly, the research has shown that the most critical factor in successful education programs is the quality of the teacher. We must give our teachers the best education, the best facilities, the best technology, ongoing on-target professional development, and salaries that reflect their value to society if our nation is to remain a leading moral, economic, cultural, and democratic force in the 21st century.

No less than Thomas Jefferson declared that a nation cannot be both ignorant and free. Therefore, we need to recognize all educators for the great value they bring to our society. Otherwise, we will continue to lose them to business and industry and shortages will become even more intense as enrollments climb and fewer people move into the field.

- **Adequate resources are focused on the weakest learners.**

Federal programs such as Title I of the Elementary and Secondary Education Act, which helps advance education for the disadvantaged, and IDEA, which supports education for individuals with disabilities, have made a positive difference. But those programs have not been adequately funded.

According to AASA Director of Government Relations Bruce Hunter, GAO has found that states have not adequately targeted funding to economically disadvantaged students. In the 21st century, communities and the nation may finally realize that the cost of neglect runs high. So do the benefits of investing in all children, whatever their social, economic, or other status.

- **Additional incentives encourage the best teachers to work with the most disadvantaged children.**

When people are finger-pointing, they often express concern that the best teachers are assigned to teach the most advantaged students while novice teachers are assigned to the most disadvantaged children, who are often the most difficult to educate. This situation presents double jeopardy. First, disadvantaged children may suffer further learning setbacks despite the heroic efforts of their teachers. Second, many first-year teachers placed in this situation lose heart and leave the profession. Therefore, the 21st century will likely, of necessity, realize the need for added incentives to attract a greater number of master teachers to dedicate their talents to disadvantaged children.

- **An investment in basic and applied research supports educational reform.**

Further basic and applied research is needed to uncover the essential requirements for educational reform. Schools must be able to systematically apply research findings to practice. During the last three decades of the 20th century, we have applied many effective learning theories supported by research to schools here and there. It has been much more difficult, however, to scale up these findings to benefit all children and schools.

- **Incentives are provided to attract members of minority groups into the teaching profession as educators and role models.**

For several decades, various groups have attempted to attract talented people from minority groups into careers in teaching and administration. While some progress has been made, few are satisfied with the numbers who have answered the call. As we move into the 21st century, we will be a nation of "minorities." Role models will continue to be important for our students.

- **Teachers are paid based on merit.**

Merit pay has been a contentious issue in U.S. schools. Yet, there are those who feel teachers and administrators should be rewarded for outstanding accomplishment. Some teachers find the lock-step salary schedules that exist in most school systems inadequate though dependable.

As we wrap up the 20th century and move forward into the 21st, teachers who have been in the classroom for years hear stories about their graduates making tens of thousands of dollars, straight out of college. On the other hand, it might take them a decade or more to reach that level. In some cases, frustration sets in and teachers leave the classroom. Too often, those who have been educated to teach move directly into business and industry, government, or other professions, never setting foot in a classroom following their graduation. Forecaster Marvin Cetron predicts that as the roles of teachers change, discussions of additional pay scales that reward merit may find their way back onto the agenda.

- **Technology replaces textbooks as the primary instructional medium.**

Texas was the first state to adopt a multimedia product instead of a textbook. As more effective technology products become available, we can anticipate that school and school system publishing, both in hard copy and electronic formats, will become even more cost-effective and efficient, with on-time delivery of tailor-made educational materials. While books, textbooks, and other printed resources are here to stay, software is offering increasingly valuable and targeted alternatives. This situation will spur heated discussions as schools and school systems develop their budgets in the 21st century.

ADDITIONAL CHARACTERISTIC: TARGETED FUNDING

An additional characteristic identified by the Council of 21 related to targeted funding includes a suggestion that principals and assistant principals assume some teaching responsibilities to improve administrator-faculty relations and gain an better grounding for administrative decisions.

Section 3: Research-Based Improvement

In an economy where the only certainty is uncertainty, the only sure source of lasting competitive advantage is knowledge.

I. Nonaki 1991

Historically, educational research in the United States has been under-funded. While some research has produced valuable insights into effective teaching and learning, much of it has not been adequately targeted. Contemporary research that has brought about change or at least healthy debate include recent studies about the relationship between time and learning, brain growth and development, and early childhood education. Growing numbers of studies are also exploring the effect of technology on student achievement. A research topic suggested by the Council of 21 relates to how schools can make their academic content more challenging and motivating.

The following characteristics of 21st century schools and school systems, related to research as an important guide for education, were identified by the Council of 21:

- **Educators use research that helps improve student achievement as a driving force in the school system.**

"Research should help drive our decisions," says former National Teacher of the Year Terry Dozier.

"We need a balance of hard and soft, qualitative and quantitative research," adds teacher Kimberly Cetron.

In the 21st century, schools and school systems will feel pressure, internally and externally, to assign a person to interpret and suggest applications of social science research. Many school systems will have a sophisticated research department whose mission will be to interpret research for teachers, administrators, board members, and the community, and much of that research will help schools and school systems decide how to improve student achievement.

Business and industry spend a significant amount on research and development. This is not true of education, where it may be needed most.

- **From research and best practices, educators design, implement, and evaluate improved learning experiences for students.**

All aspects of curriculum and instruction must have an expanded research base that can be readily explained to an ever more sophisticated and education-conscious community. This research will help drive program design, implementation, and evaluation.

- **Basic and applied research support education reform.**

Research has been mentioned as a requisite in nearly every part of this study. The Council of 21 sees research as essential in shaping schools into institutions capable of preparing students for a global knowledge/information age. They further believe a significant body of research is available and can be used instantly. For example, a new body of brain-growth research is available because of EMR, CAT scans, and other digital technology. Researchers are learning more about basic language development and about visual perception that can be related to the way we teach young children. And that is just the tip of the iceberg. However, major reform that is either knee-jerk or simple tinkering should be avoided until research-driven innovations are implemented and evaluated over time.

- **Teachers are able to conduct, analyze, and apply research in their classrooms.**

Teachers must have knowledge and experience in conducting, analyzing, and applying the findings of research. However, a suggestion to make "teacher-as-researcher" a requirement for recertification met with mixed reviews from the Council of 21. "Just as we don't want doctors doing research on their patients, we should not expect teachers to do research on their students," declares Fege. "However," he says, "teachers should have a consummate knowledge and grasp of research and the ability and freedom to apply it."

Teacher Sue Walters says, "Teacher-as-researcher projects should be supported but not mandated. Otherwise, you may get compliance but not a lot of learning, and that misses the whole point."

- **New research models are developed that deliver more definitive results.**

The bottom line for education research is better results in the classroom—higher student achievement. Often, research focuses on short-term achievement by students. Longer term longitudinal studies are fewer and further between. The Council of 21 calls for long-term, more definitive studies and views grounding improvement decisions on sound research as a crucial act of school system leadership.

Studies of Effective Educational Reform

The New American Schools program, which is both federally and privately funded, has demonstrated and documented practices in a number of districts that have made significant progress developing new models for schools. The National Science Foundation has underwritten a number of statewide systemic change programs in science and mathematics. The U. S. Department of Education has funded Technology Challenge Grants. NASA has funded the NASA Classroom of the Future. All of these efforts have yielded some insight into what a school of the future might look like.

The Educational Development Corporation (EDC) of New York City has conducted some long-term studies of reform movements and teacher uses of technology, among other things. Margaret Honey conducted a classic study of the time it takes for a teacher to incorporate computer technology into the daily activities of a class. She also looked into the time it takes for teachers and other professionals to adjust to and master new technologies. Her study indicates that it takes three years before master teachers are able to use computers in a systematic manner on a daily basis.

EDC is currently studying several school systems on a long-term basis. One notable study focuses on Union City, N.J., a highly mobile community with a student enrollment of 10,000. Ten years ago the school system was having so many problems that the state of New Jersey was threatening to take it over. Today, the system has a model program with a high degree of success. The population is predominantly Hispanic, with many new immigrant families from Central and South America. The degree of mobility has lessened as the schools have improved and more families want to remain in Union City.

As it studied Union City's reform efforts, EDC found the following characteristics:
- The schools have a clear educational mission that was agreed upon by administrators, teachers, parents, and the business community.
- Professional development has been designed to help senior education staff effectively pursue the new directions.
- Teachers have agreed to a high level of participation.
- Strong family participation is encouraged.
- The reform effort provides educational programs for adults as well as children.
- Business partnerships, especially with IBM and Bell Atlantic, have helped support the effort.
- The district has received local, state, and national community support and press coverage.
- The mayor, governor, and U.S. president have all recognized the accomplishments of this school system.

A very important factor in the Union City story is its news coverage and the inclusion of all aspects of the community. Because of the news coverage, the community has begun to believe in its schools and has gained confidence that its children can achieve a better life through their educational accomplishments.

CHAPTER 12

Putting this Study to Work

This is not just another study to place on the shelf.

Preparing Schools and School Systems for the 21st Century is not just another study to place on the shelf. It suggests action by school systems and communities as they work toward preparing students for a global knowledge/information age.

We suggest two approaches school and community leaders might take in putting this study to work, knowing full well that creative people will conceive of other approaches that might prove even more effective.

Alternative #1: Conduct Your Own 21st Century Study

Consider conducting a study similar to the one we've conducted that will result in specific recommendations for your school or school system (see the Introduction for more details about our process). Steps might include:

- Appoint a Council of 21, which is representative of your community.
- Ask members of the Council to study this report.
- Make clear that results of your Council's work will not be a directive, but a series of characteristics (brief descriptions) of schools and school systems capable of preparing students for a global knowledge/information age. These characteristics will provide a framework and valuable information as the school system plans for the future. Remember that one purpose of this approach is to engage staff and community in the discussion and to benefit from their thinking.

- Hold a full-day meeting of the group at a significant community location. Ask local sponsors to cover any costs associated with the meeting and follow-up activities.
- Using a facilitated process, ask small groups to identify characteristics of schools and school systems capable of preparing students for a global knowledge/information age. Then, ask the full Council to group those characteristics into workable categories.
- Compose a survey listing the characteristics identified by your local Council of 21.

POSSIBLE SURVEY FORMAT
IDENTIFYING AND SORTING CHARACTERISTICS OF 21ST CENTURY SCHOOLS

Characteristic	Possible Impact (circle one)			Comments
(Please circle your top 21 choices.)	High	Medium	Low	
(Example characteristic) The definitions of "school," "teacher," and "learner" are reshaped by the digital world.	H	M	L	

Please suggest characteristics you believe should be added to our list.

_____

_____

_____

_____

- Appoint an expanded Council of Advisers, perhaps another 21 community representatives, and a representative group of school system staff, perhaps another 21, to complete the survey by placing the characteristics in some priority. The expanded group, now more than 60, will select the 21 characteristics they think will be most important as your school or school system moves into the 21st century. Their selections should come from across all categories.
- On that same survey, ask respondents to indicate the possible impact of all characteristics—high, medium, or low—on the ability of the school or school system to prepare students for a global knowledge/information age. Also request comments on any or all of the characteristics and ask participants to suggest any characteristics that might not have been mentioned.
- At every step in the process, participants should be reminded that this study is not intended to limit what the school system is doing or to simply "fix" the current system. It is devoted solely to "identifying characteristics of schools

and school systems capable of preparing students for a global knowledge/information age."

- Appoint a group to tabulate results and prepare a report for the superintendent.
- Share the results with all school staff. Then, present results of the study to the school board, to school parent and advisory groups, to community organizations, to students, and to the community at large through your newsletter, web page, the news media, and targeted presentations. Always ask for questions, concerns, and suggestions for improvement. What is important is to stimulate an ongoing discussion that can help inform planning and decision making.
- Produce graphic displays of the top 10 or 20 characteristics that can be posted in schools and school system offices.
- Make the results one part of the planning process as you prepare your schools and school system for the 21st century.
- Work to ensure systemwide and communitywide commitment to pursuing selected characteristics, remembering that professional development and effective internal and external communication will be needed to sustain your efforts.
- Enlist the help of parent, business, professional, and other community leaders in supporting your 21st century program.
- Remind staff and community members that this process, on the eve of a new century and a new millennium, is an act of leadership on behalf of children and education.

Alternative #2: Hold a Conference to Determine Next Steps

Consider holding a conference involving staff and community to discuss and even debate the characteristics identified in *Preparing Schools and School Systems for the 21st Century* and to provide advice about moving forward with plans for your 21st century schools.

- Identify up to 60 representatives from your community and staff to meet in a conference setting. You might also want to involve students. (If the number is, for example, 60, you might call it the Council of 60.)
- Before the meeting, ask members of the Council to study this report, choose 1 conference facilitator, and select 10 Council members to act as small-group facilitators and another 10 to act as recorders during the meeting.
- Convene a meeting of the group in a significant community location. A sponsor might cover the cost of this activity as a demonstration of social responsibility.

- At the full-day meeting, devote at least a half-day to discussing and debating the merits of certain characteristics identified in *Preparing Schools and School Systems for the 21st Century.*
- After a suitable introduction to rally participants around the importance of the effort, ask that groups of perhaps 6 people each identify the 10 characteristics from the study that they feel are most important to the future of their school or the school system. Each group should be pre-assigned a motivated facilitator and recorder who keeps participants engaged and on track. (You might either ask these groups to confine their discussions to the 16 major characteristics found in Chapter 1 or the more than 200 characteristics found throughout the report.)

POSSIBLE MEETING FORMAT

In Advance: Ask Council members to read this report. Select 1 conference facilitator, 10 small-group facilitators, and 10 recorders.

8:30 a.m.	**Refreshments and Conversation**
9:00 a.m.	**Kickoff Remarks, Superintendent.** *(Superintendent explains that this is not a review of the school system but an opportunity to help identify the characteristics of the schools and school systems that will be needed to prepare students, not for the industrial age, but for a global knowledge/information age.)*
	Superintendent introduces the conference facilitator and individual group facilitators.
9:30 a.m.	Working with a facilitator and a recorder, 10 groups of 6 people each identify 10 characteristics from *Preparing Schools and School Systems for the 21st Century* that they would like their local school system to consider.
10:45 a.m.	**Break**
11:00 a.m.	**Plenary Session.** Conference facilitator hears reports from each of the groups on the 10 characteristics they have identified.
12 Noon	**Lunch**
	(During lunch, facilitators review reports from the 10 groups and compile a list of the 20 most frequently mentioned characteristics. If possible, this process should be supported by technology.)
1:15 p.m.	**Plenary Session.** The group reconvenes to receive either a brief Power Point or transparency display of the top characteristics. If possible, provide each participant a printout of the list.

1:30 p.m.	Two of the 20 characteristics are assigned to each of the 10 work groups.

> *The groups receive and work toward group consensus on the following questions, presented on worksheets:*
>
> **Example Characteristic #1: Students, schools, the school system, and the community are connected around-the-clock with each other and with the world thorough information-rich, interactive technology.**
>
> • What is the school system currently doing related to this characteristic?
>
> • What could or should the school system be doing related to this characteristic?
>
> • What steps should be considered in getting from where we are to where we want to be?
>
> • After reviewing our suggestions, can we think of anything we have overlooked?
>
> • What formal or informal barriers might stand in the way of implementing the suggestions?
>
> • What groups or publics will need to understand or be involved if the suggestions are to be successfully implemented?
>
> • What theme or rallying cry would you suggest in communicating the importance of pursuing your suggestions?

3:00 p.m.	**Break**
3:15 p.m.	**Plenary Session.** Each group provides a brief report on its work. *Time is proscribed so that all groups can report, and legible worksheets are turned in to the conference facilitator.*
3:50 p.m.	Superintendent expresses thanks and again explains next steps.
4:00 p.m.	**Adjourn**

Here are possible steps for meeting follow-up:

• Within 48 hours, provide a report to all participants, members of the staff, and the school board. Share results with parent and advisory groups, community organizations, students, and the community at-large through your newsletter, web page, the news media, and targeted presentations.

• Make clear that the information, ideas, and recommendation emerging from the conference will be considered as one of several resources in planning as the school system works toward preparing students for a global knowledge/information age.

- Consider making more in-depth presentations to students, staff, parent, business, professional, and other community groups, making clear that the school system has undertaken this effort as an act of leadership as it plans for preparing its students for the 21st century.

* * *

Again, these approaches are presented only to stimulate thinking and should be modified or replaced with other activities that might be even more appropriate for various communities and their school systems.

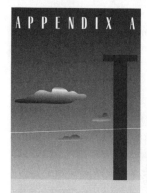

The Challenge

The Council of 21 accepted our challenge and identified more than 200 characteristics of schools and school systems capable of preparing students for a global knowledge/information age. However, a further challenge lies ahead as educators and communities consider how to sort through these characteristics and bring them to life as actual descriptions of their schools.

As part of the research design and data analysis for this study, the top 50 characteristics were identified from across all categories, based on weighted rank order of importance and possible impact—high, medium, or low. The Council of 21 also speculated on when they thought these characteristics would become commonplace in the nation's schools. Their choices for any given characteristic's implementation time were: happening now; short term—1 to 3 years; medium-term—4 to 6 years; long-term—7 or more years; and never.

As a researcher, I found it interesting that several of the highly rated characteristics, considered to be of potentially high impact in 21st century schools and school systems, received a significant number of "never" votes. Council members' views that certain things will never happen could be based on concern about financial support, their own experience in attempting change, or other factors.

Educators and other community leaders will likely need to change attitudes as they attempt to move these items from the never category and create plans for their implementation in schools and school systems.

Characteristics that had a good showing in priority and impact, while drawing a significant number of "never-happen" comments include:

- Adequate and equally distributed funding is available to provide high-quality education for all children—regardless of the relative worth of the surrounding neighborhood.
- Teacher-as-researcher initiatives are required for certification.
- All students and teachers have equal access to technology at home and school, with adequate support.
- Salaries of teachers, principals, and superintendents are commensurate with their great worth in our diverse society.
- Adequate resources are focused on the weakest learners to ensure that everyone meets established learning standards and goals.
- School systems have a secure and adequate source of resources—fiscal, material, and human.
- Additional incentives (monetary and otherwise) are used to attract and retain the highest quality teachers to work with the poorest children.
- Programs/practices are introduced only after there is compelling, not simply anecdotal, evidence of their effectiveness.

Harvey Long
21st Century Project Consultant

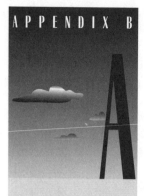

Advancing American Education

A Thumbnail Historical Perspective

When pioneer settlers first started coming to the "New World," they brought with them the concept that all people should be able to read. After all, the Bible had been printed and was widely available to anyone who wanted to personally explore its religious and ethical teachings. It might be said the earliest schools certified that children had a grounding in reading and fairly basic math, and that they had explored some of the moral and ethical rules of what was then thought to be important to a civilized world.

Thomas Jefferson was one of America's first education reformers. He believed education is essential to maintaining a democracy and that it serves as a foundation for freedom. Even though Jefferson was one of its framers, the Constitution of the United States does not directly address education. As a result, authority for schools rests with the states, which generally delegate day-to-day operation of schools to local school boards. States must ensure that their public schools are open to all children. The federal role in education operates on a broader plane.

Beginning in 1836, the federal government began looking after its obligations to students with special needs, and created an elementary school for the hearing impaired in the District of Columbia. That was followed, in the 1860s, by creation of the American Printing House for the Blind, Gallaudet University, and Howard University. During this period and earlier, however, slavery deprived legions of people of formal education.

More recently, the federal government, through Public Law 94-142 and IDEA, has established firm guidelines for meeting the needs of students with disabilities. In the 1960s, the federal government passed into law the Elementary and Secondary Education Act. Title I of that law supports education for disadvantaged children. Other programs have followed, though few, if any, have been funded at promised levels. While equal opportunity programs continue to generate debate, the nation seems firmly committed to providing education for all.

The nation was jolted by the coming of the Industrial Revolution in the mid 1800s. Jobs were becoming more complex, and workers needed to know how to read, write, do complex mathematical computations, and understand fundamental scientific concepts. It was during this period that educator Horace Mann convinced the nation that universal public education benefited not just students, but society as well. This period could be described as a time of certifying students as capable members of the workforce.

During a wave of intense immigration beginning in the late 1800s, a new high school was opening in the country every day. Education seemed to be the anchor for an industrial age, but schools were having a hard time keeping up. Land grant colleges were developed. Vocation education programs came on line. Even a forerunner of our present U.S. Department of Education was formed, staffed by three people responsible for collecting data and reporting to Congress on the condition of education in the nation.

As the nation fast became a microcosm of the world, with its schools focusing more and more on getting students ready for the workforce and life in U.S. society, a celebrated Committee of 10, chaired by Harvard President Charles Eliot, made recommendations for U.S. education in the 20th century. The Committee sought to "counteract a narrow and provincial spirit" and to "prepare the pupil...for enlightened and intellectual enjoyment." Also high on the agenda was educating students "to exercise a salutary influence upon the affairs of the country."

In 1918, the National Education Association's Commission on the Reorganization of Secondary Education wrote, in its now famous report, "The Seven Cardinal Principles," with help from the American Association of School Administrators, then the Department of the Superintendence of the NEA. The Seven Cardinal Principals were: health, command of fundamental processes, worthy home-membership, vocation, citizenship, worthy use of leisure, and ethical character.

Following World War II, the G.I. Bill ushered in an age of scientific and math education. After the Soviet Union launched Sputnik in 1957, the National Defense Education Act helped produce a generation of people so adept in science that they created technologies now transforming the world.

As we move into the 21st century, what we expect of our schools is cumulative. Schools are still expected to produce ethical, moral, civilized people who can help us sustain our democracy. They are expected to prepare students for employability. They are expected to prepare a new wave of immigrants for life in America. And as demands increase, expectations grow, and life accelerates, our schools are expected to produce people who can effectively lead us into a global knowledge/information age.

This thumbnail sketch is not intended to paint a thorough picture of the history of education in the United States, but simply to let us know that the transformation expected of us is not new. It is simply one of the great benefits and ongoing challenges of living in a free and dynamic society—a society we can only keep that way through sound education.

Frank Withrow
21st Century Project Writer

This study, *Preparing Schools and School Systems for the 21st Century*, and its companion study, *Preparing Students for the 21st Century*, are landmarks in our education history. They provide not a resting place but a platform for launching our students into an exciting new age.

References and Resources

Publications

The American Institute of Architects. (October 1998). "Reinvigorating Our Schools." Washington, DC: Author.

Christie, A. (1977). *An Autobiography. The Agatha Christie Mystery Collection.* Hicksville, N.Y.: Bantam Books.

Decker, L., G. Gregg, and V. Decker. (1994). *Getting Parents Involved in Their Children's Education.* Arlington, Va.: AASA.

Educational Research Service. (1998). *Comprehensive Models for School Improvement: Finding the Right Match to Make it Work.* Arlington, Va.: Author.

Field, D. (May/June 1998). "The Next Best Thing to Being There." *Teacher Magazine* 48-51.

Gardner, H. (1993). *Multiple Intelligences: The Theory in Practice.* New York: Basic Books.

Hoyle, J., F. English, and B. Steffy. (1998). *Skills for Successful 21st Century Schools Leaders.* Arlington, Va.: AASA.

Johnson, N. *The Knowledge Economy: The Nature of Information in the 21st Century.* (1993). Institute for Information Studies, Northern Telecom Inc. And The Aspen Institute.

Negropointe, N. (1995). *Being Digital.* New York: Alfred A. Knopf.

Nonaki, I. (November-December 1991). "The Knowledge Creating Company." *Harvard Business Review.* 96-110.

Pauker, R. (1987). *Teaching Thinking and Reasoning Skills.* Arlington, Va.: AASA.

Rowe, M. (February 1974). "Wait-Time and Rewards as Instructional Variables." *Journal of Research and Science Teaching.*

Schwahn, C. and W. Spady. (1998). *Total Leaders.* Arlington, Va.: AASA.

Spady, W. (1998). *Paradigm Lost: Reclaiming America's Future.* Arlington, Va.: AASA.

Sweeney, J. (1988). *Tips for Improving School Climate.* Arlington, Va.: AASA.

Uchida, D. (1996). *Preparing Students for the 21st Century.* Arlington, Va.: AASA.

Wilson, E. (1998). *Consilience: The Unity of Knowledge.* New York: Alfred A. Knopf.

Withrow, F.B. (1995). *United States Education and Instruction Through Telecommunications: Distance Learning for All Learners.* Washington, DC: Council of Chief State School Officers.

Videos

"Comprehensive School Reform Models." (1998). NCREL Video Library.

"Learn & Live." (1997). George Lucas Education Foundation. (Video and accompanying book, Patty Burness, executive editor.)

"Making After-School Count." (April 1998). Charles Stewart Mott Foundation.

Web Sites

American Association of School Administrators. <http://www.aasa.org>

Center for Educational Technologies. <http//www.cet.org>

Children's Thinking. <http//www.pointsofview.com>

Consortium for School Networking. <http://cosn.org>

Council of Chief State School Officers. <http://ccsso.org>

North Central Regions Educational Laboratory. <http://ncrel.org/csrm>

Think Quest. <http://thinkquest.org>

U.S. department of Education. <http://ed.gov>

Acknowledgments

Preparing Schools and School Systems for the 21st Century has been made possible through the hard work, dedication, and intellectual insights and stamina of dozens of individuals and organizations.

AASA expresses it thanks to Harvey Long for his astute and inspired counsel on project management and research implementation; to Benjamin Broome of George Mason University for research design; to Arnold Fege, president of Public Advocacy for Kids, who served as a consultant and facilitator at the Council of 21 Mount Vernon Conference; and to Dane Fountain, Joseph Casello and Kenneth Mcllvoy of the George Mason University Graduate School. We also wish to express our thanks to video producer Gulden Fox, photographer Marshall Cohen, and stenographer Kenneth Elkin who recorded the sounds, images, and ideas generated at the Mount Vernon Conference.

In addition, we acknowledge David Keefe of America Tomorrow for technical assistance; Lou Kerestesy of Hyper-Text Communications for data analysis; Luann Fulbright for research assistance and counsel; Darlene Pierce, director of development for AASA, for her guidance in preparation for the Council of 21 meeting; and Sharon Cannon and Shari Carney, AASA senior administrative assistants for their outstanding support.

The Council of 21 meeting took on historic significance because of the interest and leadership of James Rees, resident director of Mount Vernon, and Sandra Robinette.

We express our deepest gratitude to members of the Council of 21, the Council of Advisers, and representatives of gravity-breaking school systems for so freely sharing their insights and experiences, which form the very substance of this study. In addition, we were sustained by the support and wise counsel of AASA Executive Director Paul Houston, 1997-98 AASA President Karl Hertz, and 1998-99 AASA President Daniel Domenech. Our thanks to Frank Withrow who developed the initial manuscripts for this publication, assisted by Margaret Withrow, and to Gary Marx, then executive director of the AASA Leadership for Learning Foundation, now a senior consultant for AASA and president of the Center for Public Outreach, who conceived of and provided overall leadership for this study.

The financial support and true spirit of partnership provided by AMP Incorporated and the Electric Power Research Institute (EPRI) have fueled this project. We believe that these far-sighted organizations have demonstrated a keen sense of social responsibility and that their contributions will provide a platform for the creation of a new system of education for the new millennium.

EPRI is one of America's oldest and largest research consortia, with some 700 member utilities and an annual research budget of $400 million. EPRI's mission is to deliver science and technology to make the generation, delivery, and use of electricity affordable, efficient, and environmentally sound. AMP is the world's leading supplier of electrical and electronic connectors and interconnections systems.

Our special thanks are extended to the following AMP Incorporated executives who played a direct supporting role in this process: James E. Marley, retired chairman of the Board; Philippe Lemaitre, corporate vice-president and chief technology officer; William Boyd, account manager; Albert Edwards, director of marketing of the Premise Cabling and LAN System Services Division; and Michael Ratcliff, director of external communication.

We are especially grateful to EPRI members and staff for providing technical advice and counsel, including: Bruce Lindsay, EPRI project manager; Karl Johnson, original EPRI project manager; Samuel DeLay of theTennessee Valley Authority, chair of the EPRI K-12 Committee; Ronald Niebel of the American Electric Power Co., vice-chair of the EPRI K-12 Committee; Elizabeth Kimmel, of the PECO Energy Co., chair of the Education/Government Committee; Kim Hart of Hart, McMurphy & Parks, support contractor to EPRI; and to the more than 700 member utilities who provided funding support.

EPRI's utility sponsors for the 21st century project included the following project leaders: Tennessee Valley Authority; American Electric Power Co.; TU Electric/Lone Star Gas; PECO Energy Co.; Illinois Power Co.; Commonwealth Edison Co.; Consolidated Edison Co. of New York, Inc.; New York Power Authority; Potomac Electric Power Co.; Allegheny Power; Houston Lighting and Power Co.; and Entergy. Additional utilities that provided funding support include: Alliant Utilities; Anchorage Municipal Light & Power; Arkansas Electric Cooperative Corp.; B.C. Hydro; Baltimore Gas & Electric; Buckeye Power, Inc.; Central and Southwest Services, Inc.; Central Hudson Gas and Electric Corp.; Chugach Electric Assn., Inc.; Sinergy; City Public Service; Dairyland Power Cooperative; Delmarva Power and Light Co.; Duquesne Light Co.; East Kentucky Power Coop., Inc.; EnerVision; General Public Utilities Corp.; Golden Valley Electric Assn., Inc.; Grant County Public Utilities District; Green Mountain Power; Hawaiian Electric Co., Inc.; Hetch Hetchy Water & Power; Hoosier Energy Rural Electric Coop., Inc.; Idaho Power Co.; Jackson County REMC; Kansas City Power & Light Co.; Lincoln Electric System; Madison Gas & Electric Co.; Montana Power Co.; Nebraska Public Power District; Northern Indiana Public Service Co.; Northern States Power Co.; Omaha Public Power District; Orange & Rockland Utilities, Inc.; Otter Tail Power Co.; Palo Alto Electric Utility; Platte River Power Authority; Public Service Co. of New Mexico; Public Service Electric and Gas Co.; Richmond Power and Light; Snohomish County Public Utility District #1; Southern Indiana Gas & Electric Co.; St. Joseph Light and Power Co.; Tacoma Public Utilities; Tri-State G&T Association, Inc.; United Power Association; UtiliCorp United, Inc.; and Wisconsin Public Service Corp.

AASA also thanks Ginger O'Neil of GRO Communications for her editorial and production assistance and Anita Dahlman of Dahlman Middour Design for designing this publication.

Preparing Schools and School Systems for the 21st Century

Council of 21

Honorary Chair:
Senator John Glenn

Joseph Aguerrebere
Deputy Director, Education, Knowledge
 and Religion
Ford Foundation
New York, NY

Kenneth Bird
Superintendent
Westside Community Schools
Omaha, NE

Marvin Cetron
President
Forecasting International, Inc.
Falls Church, VA

Hank Courtright
Vice President
Electric Power Research Institute
Palo Alto, CA

Wadi Haddad
President
Knowledge Enterprise
Vienna, VA

Sandra K. Hamburg
Vice President & Director of Education
Committee for Economic Development
New York, NY

Stephen Heyneman
Chief, Human Resources and Social
 Policy Division
The World Bank
Washington, DC

Harold Hodgkinson
President
Center for Demographic Policy
Washington, DC

Vic Klatt
Education Policy Coordinator
Committee on Education and the
 Workforce, U.S. Congress
Washington, DC

Donald Kussmaul
Superintendent
East Dubuque School District 119
East Dubuque, IL

Stephanie Pace Marshall
President
Illinois Math & Science Academy
Aurora, IL

Floretta Dukes McKenzie
Chairman and CEO
The McKenzie Group
Washington, DC

John Merrow
The Merrow Report
New York, NY

George Nelson
Director, Project 2061
American Association for the
    Advancement of Science
Washington, DC

Arnold Packer
Professor
Johns Hopkins University
Baltimore, MD

Gary Rowe
President
Rowe, Inc.
Atlanta, GA

Robert Slavin
Professor
Johns Hopkins University
Baltimore, MD

Eric Smith
Superintendent
Charlotte-Mecklenberg Public Schools
Charlotte, NC

Michael Sullivan
Executive Director
Agency for Instructional Technology
Bloomington, IN

Kay Toliver
Teacher
P.S. 72, East Harlem Technical
Middle School
New York, NY

Sandra Welch
Senior Vice President of Education
PBS
Alexandria, VA

Preparing Schools and School Systems for the 21st Century

Council of Advisers

The Council of Advisers joined the Council of 21 and representatives of gravity-breaking school systems in completing a two-round Delphi survey devoted to identifying the characteristics of schools and school systems capable of preparing students for a global knowledge/information age.

Monica Bradsher
MPB Associates
Arlington, VA

Kimberly Cetron
Teacher
Fairfax, VA

Terry Dozier
Special Advisor to the Secretary
U.S. Department of Education
Washington, DC

Leilani Lattin Duke
Former Director
Getty Education Institute for the Arts
Los Angeles, CA

Lorraine Edmo
Executive Director
National Indian Education Association
Alexandria, VA

Arnold Fege
President
Public Advocacy for Kids
Annandale, VA

Stephen Friedlander
President
HMFH Architects, Inc.
Cambridge, MA

Mary Gorman
Education Development Manager
Xerox Corporation
Los Angeles, CA

Kenji Hakuda
Professor
Stanford University
Stanford, CA

Paul Heckman
Consultant
Santa Monica, CA

Harold Howe II
Former U.S. Commissioner of
Education, Harvard Professor
Hanover, NH

Bill Ingram
School Board Leader
Baltimore, MD

Jim Kelly
President
National Board for Professional
  Teaching Standards
Southfield, MI

Callie Langohr
Guidance Counselor
Flathead High School
Kalispell, MT

Philippe Lemaitre
Corporate Vice President
  & Chief Technology Officer
AMP Incorporated
Harrisburg, PA

Ernest Longoria
Principal
Burbank High School
San Antonio Public Schools
San Antonio, TX

Carol Mosely-Braun
United States Senator
Washington, DC

Huong Tran Nguyen
Teacher
Long Beach, CA

Les Omotani
Superintendent
West Des Moines Community Schools
West Des Moines, IA

Steve Ouskoui
Student
Stanford University
Stanford, CA

Charles Quigley
Executive Director
Center for Civic Education
Calabasas, CA

Dorothy Rich
President
Home and School Institute
Washington, DC

Sophie Sa
Executive Director
Panasonic Foundation
Secaucus, NJ

Philip Schlecty
President
Center for Leadership in School Reform
Louisville, KY

Mary Ann Sonntag
Principal
Konnoak Elementary School
Winston-Salem, NC

William Spady
President
Breakthrough Systems
Dillon, CO

Nancy Stover
President
Your Choice TV
Englewood, CO

Elaine Sullivan
Principal
Hernando High School
Brooksville, FL

Sue Walters
Teacher
Wells Junior High School
Kennebunk, Maine

Grace Williams
Teacher
Carter G. Woodson Elementary School
Jacksonville, FL

John Wycoff
Vice President
LSW Architects
Vancouver, WA

Preparing Schools and School Systems for the 21st Century

Gravity-Breaking Schools and School Systems

More than 20 gravity-breaking schools and school systems, representative of the hundreds already taking strides in preparing for the 21st century, participated in the Council of 21's two-round Delphi survey. They are:

Academy School District #20
Colorado Springs, Colorado
Donald Fielder, Superintendent

Offers a 15 school choice option, champions accountability, and is a leader in creative funding and incentive savings.

Camp Hill School District
Camp Hill, Pennsylvania
Cornelius Cain, Superintendent

A leader in technology, takes risks in exploring new approaches to learning, engages in a corporate partnership that enables teachers to learn, dream, and apply what technology can do for students.

Central Oahu School District
Miliani, Hawaii
Aileen Hokama, Superintendent

Embraces a vision for change to prepare students for the 21st century, including school- community-based management, a learning improvement process, a focus on inclusion and community-building, a site-based continuum of care at each school, school-to-work, and interdisciplinary plans.

Chatham County School District
Savannah, Georgia
Virginia Edwards, Superintendent

Dedicated to "a journey to excellence." A "third grade reading warranty" is aimed at taking students to new heights.

Chittenden South Schools
Hinesburg, Vermont
Curtis Hinds, Superintendent

Has developed performance indicators, correlated to state standards, for student use of information technology. Offers a technologically integrated curriculum.

Collinsville Community School District #10
Collinsville, Illinois
Thomas Fegley, Superintendent

A highly interactive school district. High school staff prepares students for life in a high-tech society.

David Douglas School District #40
Portland, Oregon
Barbara Rommel, Superintendent

"Learning today for living tomorrow." Through partnerships with businesses, colleges, and governmental agencies, students prepare for their futures.

Douglas County School District
Minden, Nevada
Pendery Clark, Superintendent

*Raising standards for **all** students. Graduates in 2002 will be competent in seven basic skills, including technology and "employability."*

Einstein Elementary School, Chicago Public Schools
Chicago, Illinois
Phyllis Tate, Principal

The plan becomes a reality. For the poorest and the learning disabled, technology bridges the gap to becoming the best.

City of Hammond Schools
Hammond, Indiana
David Dickson, Superintendent

On the road from school-to-work. Restructuring for partnerships and employability in the 21st Century.

Hilton Central School District
Hilton, New York
Christopher Bogden, Superintendent

A classic example in professional development. Training faculty in 21st century relationship between curriculum and how it is delivered and assessment.

Indian Prairie School District
Aurora, Illinois
Gail McKenzie, Superintendent

A telephone in every classroom and all buildings networked. Has voice mail, e-mail, and Internet connections for all staff, board, and students on a class-by-class basis. District and school web sites are linked to allow parents to view events, curriculum, PTA news, and student work.

Lake Worth Independent School District
Fort Worth, Texas
Klaus Driessen, Superintendent

Technology is the great equalizer. Reaching for the stars and finding them on the Internet and in the eyes of students.

Lincoln Public School District #1
Lincoln, Nebraska
Philip Schoo, Superintendent

A model for site-based management. The focus is clear — students are learning now for life in the 21st century.

Marble Falls Independent School District
Marble Falls, Texas
James Stuart, Superintendent

Implementing technology making use of student expertise. Networking to the future.

Maryville City School District
Maryville, Tennessee
Michael Dalton, Superintendent

Achieving success through a decentralized governance system. Decisions by principals; support by superintendent.

Montgomery County School District
Troy, North Carolina
Harold Brewer, Superintendent

A true, rural learning organization. Community collaboration maximizes benefits for social, emotional, and economic growth for children and families.

Murfreesboro City School District
Murfreesboro, Tennessee
Marilyn Mathis, Director of Schools

A tradition breaker. Communication among members of the board, administration, and faculty brings intense focus on students and their paths to learning.

Pittsburgh Public School District
Pittsburgh, Pennsylvania
Dale Frederick, Superintendent

A model system for professional development, basic skills instruction, and student assessment. The standards-based strategic plan serves as the springboard to major reform initiatives.

Pittsford Central School District
Pittsford, New York
John O'Rourke, Superintendent

Parental involvement yields results. Pittsford Central is not only in the community, but of the community as well. Engages in continuous improvement.

PS102Q
Glendale, New York
Harvey Sherer, Principal

With a student body representing 45 nations, integrated connectivity thrives at PS102Q. With a mission to create a technological and cultural arts curricula, this school is preparing student to be productive citizens in the 21st century.

San Juan Unified School District
Carmichael, California
General Davie, Jr., Superintendent

Noted for strong partnerships among students, staff, parents, and community; a shared belief that all students can learn, high expectations for student achievement; effective use of proven instructional and intervention strategies; and a districtwide focus on results.